Trouble in the Classroom

W. George Scarlett and Associates

Foreword by
Sylvia Feinburg

Trouble in the Classroom

. . . .

Managing the Behavior Problems of Young Children

Jossey-Bass Publishers
San Francisco

Chapter Ten material adapted from Ballenger, Cynthia. "Because You Like Us: The Language of Control," *Harvard Educational Review*, 62:2, pp. 199–208. Copyright © 1992 by the President and Fellows of Harvard College. All rights reserved.

Chapter Thirteen epigraph from *Science of Education and the Psychology of the Child* by Jean Piaget, Translation copyright © 1970 by Grossman Publishers, Inc. Used by permission of Viking Penguin, a division of Penguin Books USA Inc.

For sales outside the United States, please contact your local Simon & Schuster International Office.

Jossey-Bass Web address: http://www.josseybass.com

 Manufactured in the United States of America on Lyons Falls Turin Book. This paper is acid-free and 100 percent totally chlorine-free.

Library of Congress Cataloging-in-Publication Data

Trouble in the classroom : managing the behavior problems of young
  children / [edited by] W. George Scarlett.
      p.   cm. —(The Jossey-Bass education series)
   Includes bibliographical references and index.
   ISBN 0-7879-1067-8 (alk. paper)
     1. Classroom management   2. Problem children—Behavior modification
     3. Behavior disorders in children.   4. Problem children—Education (Early
   childhood)   I. Scarlett, W. George.   II. Series.
   LB3013.T76   1997
   371.5'3—dc21   97-17600

HB Printing   10 9 8 7 6 5 4 3 2 1   FIRST EDITION

The Jossey-Bass Education Series

• •

For Shirley, Will, and Evan

Contents

· ·

Foreword

N̲o aspect of teaching young children is more challenging than handling behavior problems in the classroom. This is particularly true for teachers who are committed to developmental education and who recognize that the optimal handling of behavior is not simply a matter of applying a set of procedures to harness and control children but rather a delicate process of considering the unique needs of individuals as they struggle to develop a positive sense of self in a complex and confounding world. In this insightful and sensitive book, W. George Scarlett and his colleagues make explicit the developmental approach, vividly revealing the essentials of what is involved. As a clinician and developmental psychologist, Scarlett is unusual; he looks at children within the classroom context, with consideration of the learning process and a deep appreciation for teachers, including their own particular styles and temperaments. He is an astute observer of human behavior and delights in unraveling the complexities of social interaction between children and their teachers. Unlike clinicians who view the child in isolation, Scarlett is not indifferent to the power of the classroom as a force that influences behavior strategically.

Of particular significance is the way in which Scarlett goes beyond the basics of handling a particular episode or set of problems that might occur and considers other matters not always immediately associated with difficult behavior. For example, he explores the critical importance of play, specifically, fantasy and dramatic play, and reveals the way in which teachers can be influential in how they model and facilitate play for children who lack initiative and a secure sense of self. Scarlett and the other contributors to this volume help us to understand more fully that a broad array of factors influence behavior, such as the arrangement of the physical environment, the dynamics of friendship, the quality of attachment to significant adults, and the curriculum and how it relates to the struggles of an individual child. Even the way in which classroom teachers and specialists deal with one another on matters of mutual concern is considered.

One issue that is addressed directly is the way in which teachers who are committed to a developmental approach sometimes use methods that seem didactic and behavioristic. These methods are often viewed as contradictory. The contributors to this book make clear that the term *developmental* is complex and multidimensional, and that the needs of individual children require teachers to have a full range of techniques at their command. Issues of culture, temperament, and early socialization are all crucial factors that influence a teacher's decision making about how to proceed in a given situation.

In sum, although this small book deals with complicated issues related to applied child development, it does so in a direct, concise, and forthright manner, free of educational jargon. The material is rich, with vivid illustrations gathered from classrooms, making teacher-child, child-child, and even teacher-teacher interactions readily understandable to a wide range of readers.

August 1997   SYLVIA FEINBURG
                                                        MEDFORD, MASSACHUSETTS

Preface

· ·

When I began working as a consultant to early childhood programs in the 1970s, my first assignment was at a day-care center in a housing project. The teachers there had asked the local mental health agency for someone to help them with a problem. The problem was sex. Little boys and girls were doing things that seemed to involve more than the usual innocent explorations of childhood.

Since this was my first consulting assignment, I was naturally a little nervous. I was nervous also because I had no idea of what to suggest—even though I understood that no one can know beforehand what to suggest. And I am sure I was nervous because the topic was sex.

So, I arrived at the center nervous and a minute or two early as teachers herded children into the next room for naps. I took a seat and waited, something that bothered me since I was used to keeping to a set appointment time and holding to a schedule. But I was bothered even more when, at last, the teachers became free to sit with me but did not, when they nodded a friendly hello, paused to get themselves coffee, and (most bothersome to me) just chatted among themselves. The waiting, coupled with my nervousness and my having to sit on the tiniest of chairs, made me feel more like becoming a behavior problem than solving one.

Given my state, I was surprised that once the meeting began, it went so well. At first, the teachers and I seemed a perfect mismatch, and the classroom's problems seemed overwhelming. The problems included disorder stemming not so much from the character of the children as from the absence of a strong curriculum and a wise approach to classroom management. Furthermore, the teachers were not always responsible. For example, half way through my first year of consulting, one teacher took off with the others' paychecks.

But, eventually, it was clear that we were a match. For two years, consulting on an almost weekly basis, I taught the teachers how to address behavior problems indirectly by supporting the development of children's inner resources and by supporting the children's struggles to master developmental tasks—an approach that I would later characterize as "letting development be a cure for behavior problems." In return, they taught me how a classroom for young children can do well when it becomes a community.

This classroom was indeed a community, which more than made up for its problems. The children, though unruly at times, always seemed happy and secure in their connections to teachers and classmates. The parents, like small-town neighbors, stopped by for support and gossip. And the prodigal teacher, with what she described as "borrowed" paychecks, returned to an almost biblical welcome and the resumption of her job. I learned to not judge too quickly, and I learned that the business of caring for children actually is not business, but simply caring.

Years later, this theme of community came up in conversations between myself and a master teacher. I had been asking her to share her thoughts with me on how curricula can help children with behavior problems. I had assumed she would talk to me about materials, lessons, and projects—ways of engaging children's interests and helping them to play and work constructively. Thinking metaphorically, I reasoned that if the devil makes use of idle hands, then angels must hover about the busy. However, this teacher responded to my questions by talking to me about building a community and about ensuring that every child feels that he or she has a place in the classroom community. For her, building a community *is* the curriculum and a powerful cure for behavior problems. I agree.

This book is, in many ways, an outgrowth of those conversations and the firsthand experiences of myself and others in the classroom. Our major aim is to describe and illustrate ways to deal with behavior problems by supporting children's development and building communities in classrooms.

But these two goals present two dilemmas: first, a dilemma between meeting short-term needs for order and long-term needs for development and, second, a dilemma between meeting the needs of individual children and meeting the needs of groups of children. These dilemmas occur because what is good for maintaining order is not always good for children's development (and vice versa) and what is good for individuals is not always good for groups (and vice versa). So, a second aim of this book is to show how to manage these dilemmas.

A third aim is to define core beliefs about managing behavior problems in ways that promote children's self-control. A book on behavior problems should define a useful set of tactics for managing expectable problem behaviors, but it should do more by defining good core beliefs that provide a wellspring for generating new tactics to manage even the unexpected.

In this book, the main core belief is that behavior management for the purpose of promoting children's self-control works best when children and teachers have formed *partnerships* and when teachers have worked to *share control*. This core belief is illustrated daily by developmental educators. Over the past twenty-five years, I have sat in classrooms listening to and watching master teachers at work. I have come to the conclusion that trained, experienced early childhood educators are our nation's true experts on children's behavior problems. While others may raise their voices in anger or devise clever systems to control children, these teachers listen patiently, challenge and guide gently, and, over time, help children outgrow their behavior problems. And they succeed not so much because they have tactics for managing problem behaviors but because they adhere to this core belief about partnerships and sharing control.

In my experience, the clearest examples of the differences between these master teachers developing partnerships with children and sharing control and the majority of not-so-masterful adults controlling children emerge at group meetings in the classroom. I remember the first time I witnessed a master teacher in a kindergarten classroom when a group meeting had fallen apart. My reflex assumption was that the teacher would raise her voice, give directives, and try to physically control a child or two. But, instead, she sat back calmly and said, "We've fallen apart. What are we going to do?"

In response to the teacher's question, one child suggested she send them all to time-out. Another said the school should hire extra teachers to see to it that the children behaved. Still others gave their points of view. The teacher listened to each child's suggestion and provided respectful feedback. Gradually, she shaped the discussion so that everyone was talking not about how some outside force could control them better but how the children in partnership with the teacher could generate good rules and routines to help them control themselves. It was a wonderful performance. Such performances are not rare. They go on all the time in good classrooms for young children, and they illustrate what I mean by a core belief for thinking about behavior problems. This book, then, attempts to explain what master teachers are already doing in their classrooms.

It also attempts to show the power of a developmental approach for helping even very diverse groups of children, children from minority cultures and children with special needs. Many teachers are rightfully concerned that children who are different from the norm often end up receiving less support because their differences are misunderstood or because others focus solely on their deficiencies. These children are sometimes unnecessarily weeded out from the larger community and subjected to environments designed mostly to control them. But these children, though different, have the same basic needs as all children for support and a sense of community. In meeting their basic needs, we may have to do things differently, but we do not have to abandon a developmental approach, as this book is designed to demonstrate.

Over twelve years ago, when I began writing this book, I fully intended to write all of its chapters. But when I began, I was not as aware as I am now of how complex the task is to transform classrooms into caring and productive communities. Happily, I found others who are more knowledgeable than me about developing classrooms. So, later chapters are written mostly by others—master teachers with wonderful stories to tell. They speak in their own voices, but each voice expresses the book's developmental approach and point of view.

This strategy of approaching behavior problems as a matter of supporting the development of children's inner resources and supporting children as they struggle to master developmental tasks, developing classrooms into caring and productive communities, managing dilemmas, and acquiring core beliefs may frustrate our normal desire for simple and clear-cut solutions, approaches that attack behavior problems head-on, and that go directly to the business of managing or eliminating those problems. But if supporting children's overall development is our primary aim, we must somehow tolerate this frustration. Classrooms are complex and messy, so our approach to behavior problems should never be too simple or too clean. A developmental approach to behavior problems is neither: it addresses the complexity and the messiness of classrooms. This book is an attempt to show how.

Acknowledgments

We are grateful to the following for permitting use of the quotes introducing the four sections of this book: *Harvard Educational Review* for permission to use a phrase adapted from Lawrence Kohlberg in Kohlberg and Mayer (1972), W. W. Norton for permission to quote from Erik Erikson's (1962) book *Young Man Luther* and from Harry Stack Sullivan's (1953) book *The Interpersonal Theory of Psychiatry*, and Kappa Delta Pi for permission to quote from John Dewey's (1963) book *Experience and Education*. We are also grateful to Penguin U.S.A. for permission to quote from Jean Piaget's *Science of Education and the Psychology of the Child*, and Robert Selman for permission to quote from *Making a Friend in Youth* by Robert Selman and Lynn Hickey-Schultz. In addition, we thank Rheta DeVries for permission to publish as Chapter 7 an excerpt of Lawrence Kohlberg and Thomas Likona's (1990) chapter "Moral Discussion and the Class Meeting" from *Constructivist Early Education: Overview and Comparison with Other Programs*, and we thank *Harvard Educational Review* for permission to reprint as Chapter 10 a revised version of Cynthia Ballenger's (1992) article "Because You Like Us: The Language of Control," copyright by the President and fellows of Harvard College, all rights reserved.

August 1997   W. GEORGE SCARLETT
                                                MEDFORD, MASSACHUSETTS

The Author

. . . .

W. GEORGE SCARLETT is assistant professor of child development in the Eliot-Pearson Department of Child Development, Tufts University, and lecturer in psychology at Assumption College, Worcester, Massachusetts. He has been a member of Harvard Project Zero's research team, a consultant and researcher for Head Start since its inception, a director of a residential camp for emotionally disturbed children, and a clinical coordinator for a psychoeducational center. Currently, he coordinates training and program evaluation for Lowell Early Head Start and provides workshops for teachers on managing young children's behavior problems. He has authored numerous articles on young children's behavior problems and on play, and he is coeditor (with Fritz K. Oser) of *Religious Development in Childhood and Adolescence*.

The Contributors

CYNTHIA BALLENGER is a sociolinguist and senior project director at the Cheche Konnen Center, a National Science Foundation–funded center for science education reform and the study of linguistic minority students. She has been an early childhood teacher for many years and a consultant on issues of equality and inclusion. Her work includes articles on the uses of language in the classroom in relation to science teaching and learning. She has a long-standing interest in Haitian communities in the United States and the problems that confront Haitian students in North American schools.

MONIQUE JETTE teaches first grade in a public school. She has been a kindergarten teacher at the Tufts University Educational Day Care Center.

LAWRENCE KOHLBERG, until his death in 1987, was professor of education and director of the Center for Moral Development and Moral Education at Harvard University. He presented his theory and research on moral stage development and its implications for education in more than a hundred articles and book chapters as well as in several books, including *The Philosophy of Moral Development, The Psychology of Moral Development, The Measurement of Moral Judgment, Programs of Early Education,* and *Lawrence Kohlberg's Approach to Moral Education.*

THOMAS LICKONA is a developmental psychologist and professor of education at the State University of New York, Cortland, where he directs the Center for the 4th and 5th Rs (Respect and Responsibility). He collaborated with Lawrence Kohlberg on the application of moral development theory to the moral education of children. He is the author or editor of several books, including *Moral Development and Behavior*, *Raising Good Children*, and *Educating for Character: How Our Schools Can Teach Respect and Responsibility*.

KIM E. MYERS is director of operations for Worcester Comprehensive Child Care Services (WCCCS), Inc., a nonprofit child care agency for low- to moderate-income families. She is also director of the School Age Program and is currently working on creating a certificate program for professionals in school age programs in conjunction with Quinsigamond Community College. Her current areas of interest include children's environments, media, and Reggio Emilia's approach to education and its applications to urban school age programs.

SUSAN STEINSIECK teaches kindergarten at the Eliot-Pearson Children's School, Tufts University. In addition, she is an artist and professional singer. For many years, she sang with Benny Goodman and Scott Hamilton.

JENNIFER WICKHAM is a school counselor in the Boston Public School System. In the past she has taught emotionally disturbed children and been a member of several research teams investigating issues pertaining to mental health and education.

KRISTEN J. WILLAND teaches first grade in a public school. She has taught kindergarten at the Tufts University Educational Day Care Center. She is a member of the Phi Beta Kappa Society.

Trouble in the Classroom

Part One

. . . .

Introduction

Development [is] the aim of education.
    Lawrence Kohlberg (Kohlberg and Mayer, 1972)

In Part One, we provide an overview of a developmental approach to behavior problems. The key elements of this approach are supporting the development of children's inner resources and their struggles to master developmental tasks, developing classrooms into caring and productive communities, and accommodating diversity.

The original quote from Kohlberg and Mayer (1972) read "Development *as* the aim of education."

1

A Developmental Approach to Behavior Problems

Gilbert Ryle, a prominent philosopher, once told this story about defining key terms: A young man had just been shown around a university. He had visited all the main buildings—the library, the gym, the dorms—when he asked his guide, "But where is the university?" (Ryle, 1949). Here, our question, "Where (or what) is a developmental approach to behavior problems?" has a similar quality, and if we are not careful, we might end up like Ryle's young man. My point is that a developmental approach to behavior problems has no single, tangible element that uniquely identifies it: no set of tactics for managing behaviors, no particular curriculum, no specific classroom routine.

Like the concept of a university, a developmental approach refers to several related things. First, the term refers to developing children's inner resources, their thinking and ways of managing feelings. Second, it refers to helping children master developmental tasks. Third, it refers to developing classrooms into caring and productive communities. And, fourth, it refers to supporting development in the face of diversity.

Developing Children's Inner Resources

Many behavior problems in early childhood result from children's immature thinking and immature ways of managing feelings. That is why a developmental approach to behavior problems works to develop children's inner resources.

Guidance for Thinking

Experienced teachers often manage behavior problems by guiding young children to think more maturely. This guidance is illustrated nicely by Grace Mitchell's (1993, p. 28) advice for what to do about fighting: "You might suggest that each child bring you a chair (from opposite sides of the room). That way you will divert their attention and give yourself a moment to plan. Placing the chairs so that the children are sitting facing each other, their knees touching, you might say, 'I can see that you are both angry. When there is an argument and each person thinks that he or she is right, we need to *com-mu-ni-cate* with words instead of fists.' (It's helpful to stress each syllable when introducing a 'grown-up' word.) Help the children use words by saying, 'Joey, tell Tony why you think you are right.' . . . If Tony interrupts, explain, 'No, Tony, it's Joey's turn to talk. When he is finished, you'll have your turn.' Guide the conversation, making sure that each child has equal time to talk. Then ask, 'What do you think is the best way to settle this?'"

In Mitchell's advice, she does more than suggest ways to stop children from fighting. She suggests ways to help children *think* about alternatives to fighting, ways to problem-solve and negotiate their conflicts. All of this is heady stuff for young children, requiring adult support and a long time to practice.

Support for Managing Feelings

Experienced teachers also understand that behavior problems can result from the immature ways in which young children manage their feelings—negative feelings such as anxiety and anger, but positive feelings as well. Here is one of my favorite examples of a teacher preventing behavior problems by helping children manage their positive feelings of curiosity and excitement. In this example, the teacher was about to use a hot-air popper to make popcorn. She knew that as soon as she turned the machine on, the children would reach and grab. So, to prevent them from doing so, she had them practice controlling themselves:

> TEACHER: Are we going to touch the machine?
> CHILDREN: Nooo!
> TEACHER: Are we going to grab the popcorn as it comes out?
> CHILDREN: Nooo!
> TEACHER: Look at your hands. (She holds out her own hands, and the children do the same.) Tell them, "DON'T TOUCH!"
> CHILDREN: (in unison) "DON'T TOUCH!"

When the magical moment came, no one touched. As this example indicates, like thinking, children's management of their feelings requires a lot of adult support and a lot of practice time.

Helping Children Master Developmental Tasks

One of the main features of a developmental approach to behavior problems is the focusing on larger tasks than that of managing particular behaviors and situations, tasks that characterize a child's stage in life and that need to be mastered if a child is to thrive in the present and move on to a higher stage. Here, more than anywhere, development can be a cure for behavior problems.

What are these developmental tasks? Erikson (1950) described each stage as being organized around one major task, such as acquiring a sense of basic trust (infancy), a sense of autonomy (very early childhood), or a sense of initiative (preschool period). But stages are too complex for any one task to capture all aspects of a stage. And certain tasks remain central across stages even as they become redefined. So, I offer a longer list to give a better sense of the major developmental tasks characterizing early childhood.

Feeling Connected

Obviously, feeling secure through attachment to a caregiver is a developmental task for the infant, and, clearly, the issues of security and attachment continue into early childhood. But security and attachment take on new meanings when we speak of young children. Young children need additional sources of security, new ways of feeling connected. Young children need more than physical connections; they need psychological connections as well, connections that come from feeling understood and appreciated, from being guided, and from knowing that someone is an ally.

A child's development of these additional sources of security through feeling connected in the classroom is identified here as the first major developmental task because feeling secure about one's connections is the primary frame for good behavior. It is a powerful motive for wanting to behave. Without this feeling, children cannot begin to tolerate or manage the growing pains that accompany the long process of learning to share control with others.

Developing a Healthy Sense of Self

Infants must also develop a sense of themselves as separate, autonomous selves, selves capable of making things happen and selves with feelings. So too, young children must develop a sense of themselves as autonomous and feeling selves. But, unlike infants, their autonomy is seen more in the directed way in which they play and assert their wills, in their development of a "directed self." And their feelings often are seen more in their fantasies and words. When, for whatever reason, young children lack a sense that they can make (good) things happen and when they lack an ability to express their feelings, they can develop behavior problems.

Becoming a Constructive Player

It is obvious that play is important to young children. But not so obvious are the ways in which constructive play develops and functions to promote healthy relationships, self-control, and an ability to cope with feelings. Also not obvious is how problems in playing can lead to behavior problems. And perhaps least obvious is what teachers can do to foster play to help with behavior problems.

Making Friends

Friendship in early childhood means more than being a cooperative playmate. Friendship means identifying with another, becoming a "we" that transcends the "me." It is this kind of connecting that we need to understand when thinking about behavior problems, especially when those problems stem from not having friends or from becoming stuck in a bad friendship.

Summary

A developmental approach to behavior problems thus means fostering close relationships with children and among children so that they feel secure through feeling connected. It means fostering the development of children's sense of themselves as having direction and feelings. It means fostering children's abilities to play constructively. And it means fostering children's capacity to make healthy friendships.

The reason for emphasizing developmental tasks is this: A child who feels secure through feeling connected, who has a healthy sense of self, who plays constructively, and who has good friends cannot at the same time be a child with serious behavior problems. Therefore, by emphatically supporting development on these major tasks, teachers can be less concerned with eliminating behavior problems and more concerned with helping children outgrow them.

Developing Classrooms into Caring and Productive Communities

A developmental approach to behavior problems is sometimes assumed to focus mostly on individuals. However, the approach is much broader in scope and also emphasizes developing classrooms into caring and productive communities. This emphasis stems from the observation that the building of classroom communities can do much to prevent and manage behavior problems as well as to support children's development. Therefore, later chapters in this book focus on ways in which classrooms can be developed both to prevent behavior problems and to support children's development. These later chapters look closely at the following areas: developing a just and caring community, using the curriculum to give children a voice, and designing programming and the physical environment so as to prevent behavior problems.

Just and Caring Community

In Chapter 7, Kohlberg and Lickona focus on moral discussion and the class meeting. They clarify how making a classroom a just and caring community can be a powerful way to both prevent and manage behavior problems. For Kohlberg and Lickona, the key is helping children to "get morality on the inside," to see rules not as the decrees of outside authorities but rather as useful guides for deciding what is good and fair.

Curriculum

In Chapter 8, Susan Steinsieck and Kim E. Myers continue the discussion about developing classrooms into communities. But, in this chapter, the message is about how curriculum can give children a voice or sense of belonging. It can do so if teachers build on children's strengths and interests, making children partners in the development of curriculum. Several examples show how giving children a voice through curriculum can be a good way to address their behavior problems.

Programming and the Physical Environment

In Chapter 9, Kim E. Myers and I focus on programming and the physical environment, emphasizing the need for teachers to organize time, space, and the physical environment so as to avoid frustrating children, to orient children, and to help children become self-directed. We illustrate how even minor changes in programming and in the environment can prevent behavior problems.

Supporting Development in the Face of Diversity

All children are different. Usually, being different does not prevent a child from thriving in traditional settings. However, there are some children whose differences are salient to understanding why they do not thrive under average conditions, where teachers instruct in traditional ways. Their differences call for major accommodations by teachers. Two types of differences are discussed in this book: differences based on culture and differences based on special needs.

Children from Minority Cultures

Minority children often struggle to adjust to mainstream culture and the ways in which mainstream classrooms are run. What we in the mainstream assume to be good educational practice can be wrong for children from minority cultures. And when we educators get it wrong, the result can be behavior problems.

So, a developmental approach to behavior problems must include ways to accommodate minority groups, foremost by understanding behavior problems from the perspective of cultural differences. More specifically, a developmental approach to behavior problems must include an understanding of what it means to support development as defined within a minority child's own culture. In Chapter 10, Cynthia Ballenger describes how she managed Haitian children's behavior problems by using the Haitian "language of control."

Children with Special Needs

Children with special needs may be from the mainstream culture, but put them with good teachers in the best classrooms with the most understanding peers, and, still, some will have behavior problems. With these children, we need to prepare ourselves to abandon usual ways of sharing control, even to the point of using tactics directed more at maintaining control. But we should do this without giving up on developing their inner resources and without giving up on supporting them as they struggle to master developmental tasks. Furthermore, we should do this while including them in caring and productive communities. This approach is not easy, as Monique Jette, in Chapter 11, and Kristen J. Willand, in Chapter 12, clearly show.

These later chapters, then, put the developmental approach to the test. The authors help us see the approach more clearly and understand just how it works. That is, in meeting the challenges posed by children from minority cultures and by children with special needs, we see the developmental approach at work in some of the most difficult, real-world classroom settings.

Teachers' Styles

Over the past twenty years of consulting to early childhood programs, I have met many remarkable teachers, each with his or her own distinctive style. Each style has seemed perfectly suited to the way in which the teacher managed behavior problems. So, a developmental approach to behavior problems takes into consideration a teacher's style.

What exactly do I mean by *teacher's style*? Teaching style is difficult to define, but it is not so difficult to recognize. Consider the following examples of master teachers and their styles:

Scott and Ben had been pushing the limit all morning. Now they were definitely beyond the limit: running around the block corner, threatening to unhinge every project on their side of the classroom. The teacher, a somewhat tough but caring type who must have successfully mothered several adolescents, turned and shouted, "You blew it. Take a seat [in time-out]." They responded immediately, knowing full well they had been caught.

Laurel pleaded with her teacher, Dan, to give her the sifter that he held while playing with the group. In his best imitation of a four-year-old's somewhat whiny voice, he replied, "No. Yesterday you wouldn't share your markers, so now I won't share my sifter." To the observer's surprise, Laurel responded as if Dan were fairness personified, and she moved on to something else.

Martha, a veteran kindergarten teacher, glided about her classroom like a night nurse checking on her sleeping patients, only her children were not asleep. Three, in fact, were quarreling and about to come to blows. Still, Martha glided and still she kept her voice to a hush as she reminded them that they might find better ways to resolve their problems. The quarreling threesome stopped immediately and resumed their play so as not to wake the others.

Susan had been teaching only a few years, but already she was a real professional. There was not an ounce of laziness about her as she stooped to listen to her three year olds. Rowdy or teary children, each received the same intense audience followed by a remarkably clear, though stoical statement of reality, such as "You'll need to find someone else to play with if Lindsey and Bill want to be alone." Some parents faulted her for being too coolly detached, but not the children. The children saw and felt her listening and responded by listening too.

Each of these teachers has his or her own distinct style. And each style works to teach, support, guide, and manage because each teacher is comfortable with and confident about who he or she is as a teacher. There is no anxiety about being too tough (the first teacher), too childlike (the second), too soft (the third), or too detached (the fourth). These teachers know that the best they can do is to be themselves at their best. Teachers are individuals, and they need to be themselves and preserve their styles even as they meet the needs of children and manage their problems.

Other Approaches

This book's developmental approach to behavior problems places greater emphasis than most other approaches on sharing control with children, on locating the causes and cures of behavior problems in children's struggles to master developmental tasks, on preventing behavior problems through development of classroom communities, and on addressing the needs of children who differ from the norm. This emphasis is designed to bring us closer to helping children outgrow their behavior problems. Differences in emphases can be seen by contrasting a developmental approach to other, common approaches falling roughly within three categories: behavior modification, clinical-medical, and guidance toward positive discipline.

Behavior Modification Approaches

Behavior modification was developed in academic, research settings. Using the methods and thinking of traditional laboratory science, professionals trained in behavior modification have helped to manage serious behavior problems. Today, there are many comprehensive behavior modification programs for special populations of children.

But the kind of behavior modification used in early childhood classrooms is rarely part of a comprehensive program. In early childhood classrooms, behavior modification usually is a circumscribed approach to managing particular problem behaviors. Usually, the principles applied are simple and can be summarized as follows: "What children do is either reinforced or not reinforced by those around them. Acceptable behavior continues if it is reinforced. Similarly, problem behavior also continues if it is reinforced. Both kinds of behaviors can be extinguished if they are not reinforced" (Essa, 1983, p. 1).

There is no question that behavior modification programs have in many instances brought order out of chaos. However, there are grounds for questioning whether the kind of order at which behavior modification aims is suitable for young children in classrooms. I am particularly concerned about the inadequacy of behavior modification in meeting young children's needs for security and connection. I am concerned that the emphasis on adult control has in many cases led parents and teachers to engage in a kind of mechanical, sometimes even ill-humored, overcontrol.

There is, of course, nothing to prevent those who use behavior modification from being warm and friendly. Nevertheless, it is fair to say that the language of reinforcement and consequences is a cold language, which can have a chilling effect. The following example illustrates what I mean. Here, the teacher acts coolly as she threatens Jeff (age three) in order to get him to follow a bathroom routine:

TEACHER: Okay, children, let's line up and go to the bathroom.
JEFF: Nooo, I don't want to.
TEACHER: Jeff, you have a choice of either coming to the bathroom by yourself or my helping you.
JEFF: Nooo.
TEACHER: One, two. (Jeff reluctantly and slowly goes to the bathroom but, once there, refuses to go into a stall.)
JEFF: (screaming and whining) I don't want to go.
Teacher: Jeff, you have a choice to go to the bathroom or sit in the thinking chair.
JEFF: I don't want to go.
TEACHER: One, two. (Jeff slowly goes into a stall and just stands there.) Jeff, you have to pull down your pants and go.
JEFF: Nooo, I don't want to.
TEACHER: (with a somewhat threatening tone to her voice) You have a choice of pulling your pants down yourself or I will help you.
JEFF: Nooo.
TEACHER: One, two. (Jeff slowly pulls down his pants, pees, then toddles out of the bathroom with his pants still at his ankles.)

It is not surprising that this teacher struggled daily with Jeff, not just over the bathroom routine but over other issues as well. She won the battle over the bathroom but not the war over developing partnerships and self-control.

In behavior modification there can be what Redl and Wineman (1965, p. 228) referred to as a "perversion of motivation" and the promoting of a "business deal concept of life." Behavior modification plays on the pleasure principle and appeals to the motives of increasing personal pleasure and promoting self-interest. There is little in this approach to support children's motives for being a part of a community.

Finally, much of what we do for young children is designed not to reward but to attend to some need. As Redl and Wineman (1965, p. 229) observed, "Children need affection and full gratification of their needs, ample symbols of adult acceptance and love. . . . To tie any set of gratifications to the condition that they perform well would be like promising a child cough medicine provided he goes without coughing for a day." Here is an example of the kind of problem Redl and Wineman would have us avoid:

> At one day-care center, a toddler was having a particularly difficult time separating from his mother. Each morning, after his mother left, this toddler cried loudly and for quite a while. Thinking in terms of reinforcement, the teachers decided to extinguish the crying by ignoring the child. Their ignoring led to less crying, but the now quiet child was both apathetic and withdrawn.

Clinical-Medical Approaches

This book's developmental approach to behavior problems says virtually nothing about so-called behavior disorders of childhood, such as attention deficit with hyperactivity disorder and oppositional defiant disorder. The developmental approach does not speak the medical language of behavior disorders for several reasons: First, the language of disorders does not help identify those causes of behavior problems over which teachers have control; second, this language has little to say about what teachers should do for children; and, third, this language can dehumanize children.

Labels such as attention deficit with hyperactivity disorder and oppositional defiant disorder follow the medical tradition of, first, assessing symptoms to determine some underlying biological cause, which will, in turn, suggest a treatment. But children's behavior problems are different from medical disorders. First, patterns of problem behaviors do not clearly point to biological causes. So, for example, finding that a child is unusually active, impulsive, and inattentive does not by itself establish a biological cause. Second, and more important, patterns of problem behaviors do not by themselves suggest treatments. So, hyperactivity, impulsiveness, and inattentiveness do not by themselves clarify what teachers should do. In short, labeling in the clinical-medical tradition does not help us figure out all that we need to figure out if we are going to help children with their behavior problems.

There is the argument that labels, while not useful in explaining behavior and while not useful in suggesting treatments, are of value nonetheless because they reduce the chances that we will blame children for their problems and because they give meaning to otherwise seemingly meaningless behavior. Perhaps this is so. But without labels, we need not blame; and with labels, we still need to find meaning by looking at inner resources, developmental tasks, and whether classrooms are communities.

There is, though, a third reason this book's developmental approach does not follow the clinical-medical tradition of labeling. Labels for disorders were never intended to be labels for children. From a medical point of view, labeling a child according to his or her disorder is like saying a person with a common cold *is* a common cold. However, when using these psychiatric labels, all of us succumb occasionally to the tendency of saying "attention deficit disorder children," "autistic children," and the like. All of us occasionally look at children through their labels.

In sum, the book's developmental approach does not focus on psychiatric labels because they are not needed. Moreover, labels can make us look at children with problems more in terms of their being problems and less in terms of their being children.

Guidance Approaches to Positive Discipline

Approaches to behavior problems that fall within this category are commonly found in the literature for teachers of young children. While there are significant differences among these approaches, they share certain emphases. First, they all emphasize the importance of teachers being positive, respectful, and nurturing toward children rather than ridiculing or punishing children. For example, "Good discipline is not just punishing or enforcing rules. It is liking children and letting them see that they are liked" (Stone, 1994, p. 7). Or "Children will be kind, considerate, and generous if that is how they are treated" (Honig, 1989, p. 2).This emphasis reflects a deep respect for young children and a deep appreciation for the fact that young children have the same need to be treated with respect as any other group of human beings.

Second, they all emphasize self-esteem as necessary for children to outgrow their behavior problems. For example, "Nothing is more consistently and intimately linked to a wide variety of emotional and behavioral disturbances than is a low opinion of oneself" ("Ideas That Work with Young Children," 1988, p. 25).

Third, they all emphasize the importance of setting limits and being firm. For example, "I believe caring deeply about children means you want good-humored control and firm discipline for them. . . . I believe that children should be expected to obey adults, provided the adults are reasonable" (Stone, 1994, p. 2).

Fourth, they all emphasize the importance of guiding children. For example, "Discipline is the slow, bit-by-bit, time-consuming task of helping children to see the sense in acting in a certain way" (Hymes, in Mitchell, 1993, p. 6).

Fifth, they all emphasize classroom management. For example, "A classroom in which movement is rigidly controlled, arbitrary rules are imposed, disorganization of materials is commonplace, and little thought is given to enhancing the room's comfort and attractiveness is a nonsupportive, hostile environment. This type of space does not support the growth of mastery and self-control" (Marion, 1987, p. 63).

Clearly, these guidance approaches to positive discipline have a lot in common with this book's developmental approach—so much so that one might ask, "What's the difference?" The main difference is that this book's developmental approach demonstrates a wider variety of points of entry; that is, the approach shows there are a greater number of options for addressing behavior problems than most discussions on behavior problems would lead us to believe. These options include building close relationships between teacher and child, supporting a child's development of a healthy sense of self, helping a child become a constructive player, supporting a child's attempts to make good friendships, promoting a just and caring community, building curricula around children's interests, making helpful changes in programming, redesigning the physical environment, accommodating the child's culture, coordinating with special education, and, of course, trying new behavior management tactics. Figure 1.1 illustrates the points of entry that are discussed in this book. There are others, of course, such as the parent-teacher relationship and the need to address physiologically based problems. The challenge is to use all of our options, rather than rely on just one or two.

This emphasis on points of entry makes the developmental approach different from and more flexible than traditional guidance approaches to discipline. The developmental approach also better mirrors what goes on in early childhood classrooms where teachers bring virtually everything within their powers to bear on helping children outgrow their problems.

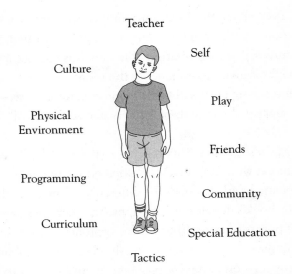

Teacher

Self

Culture

Play

Physical
Environment

Friends

Programming

Community

Curriculum

Special Education

Tactics

Figure 1.1. Points of Entry for Addressing Behavior Problems.

2

Tactics for Managing Behavior Problems

W hat should we do about hitting, biting, fidgeting, and shouting? How do we get children to sit quietly, speak kindly, and follow directions? These are all questions about tactics, about tools to manage behavior problems. Unfortunately, the answers to these questions are not simple. This chapter explains why.

There is a common belief that every behavior problem has a corresponding "right" tactic for managing the problem—sort of like the song about there being just one girl for every boy. Both the belief and song are wrong. That is not to say there are not right matches between behavior problems and tactics as well as between girls and boys. There are. But questions about tactics are also questions about matching.

There is also a common belief that holds just the opposite: "Be eclectic, mix tactics until you find what works"—a sort of hunt-and-peck approach to behavior problems. This belief too is wrong. That is not to say we should not mix tactics. We should. But we should mix tactics with an understanding of what it means for a tactic to work. In this chapter, the discussion about tactics thus focuses on these problems of mixing and matching.

Mixing Tactics

A developmental approach allows us to use almost any tactic for managing behavior problems. For example, when adopting a developmental approach, there is nothing inconsistent in a teacher's use of time-outs or reinforcements to manage behavior problems, even though these tactics are usually associated with the behavior modification approach. This notion of flexibility often gets lost in discussions where adopting an approach and using a particular set of tactics are assumed to be one and the same.

Although a developmental approach does not commit us to using a particular set of tactics, it does commit us to mixing tactics as needed to manage the two dilemmas mentioned in the Preface. The first dilemma is between meeting short-term needs for order and long-term needs for development. This dilemma can be managed in two ways. The first way is to choose tactics that serve both needs, as when Grace Mitchell (1993) guides her children both to stop fighting and to negotiate their conflict. The second way of managing this dilemma is to alternate between tactics designed primarily to control (Stone's [1994] "firm discipline") and tactics designed primarily to support development. We do not need to accomplish both goals at the same time. However, with this second way we are bound by Redl and Wineman's (1965, p. 153) law that whatever is good for maintaining order must not undermine long-term development, and whatever is good for supporting development must not undermine order. So, for example, physical punishment of children should never be used because it undermines long-term development. And, in most classrooms, nondirective play therapy should never be used because it tends to undermine order.

The second dilemma is between meeting the needs of individual children and meeting the needs of a group of children. This dilemma also can be managed either by meeting both kinds of needs simultaneously or by alternating between types of tactics designed for an individual and types designed for a group. Again, if alternation of tactics is the choice, Redl and Wineman's law applies. So, though a teacher's guidance of a child through an entire art project may help the child become a constructive player, if the rest of the class falls apart, this tactic cannot be used. And though, for most children, it may be right for a teacher to enforce a class rule that children must raise their hands before speaking at circle time, the rule is wrong for certain children who have serious speech and motor problems.

What all this means is that good teachers are not necessarily the most comfortable teachers. In fact, I mark it as a major development when a teacher goes from the comfortable state of thinking there are right tactics for particular behavior problems to the not-so-comfortable state of feeling the need to manage dilemmas.

Matching Tactics

To understand the problem of matching tactics, consider the following examples of children refusing to clean up: In one classroom, the teacher announced suddenly, "Time to clean up!" and a child in the block corner looked startled and refused. In another classroom, the teacher announced, "Five minutes to clean up," and a child in the block corner looked anxiously at his fort and refused. In still another classroom, the teacher gave a five-minute warning, and a child in the block corner grinned devilishly and refused. Each of these children exhibited the same problem behavior in that each refused to put away blocks when asked to do so. Should the teachers have used the same tactic for all three cases? A developmental approach suggests no: rather than match tactics to problem behaviors, we should match tactics to children and circumstances.

Matching Tactics to Children

The above examples can be used to illustrate what it means to match tactics to children. If we used the same tactic with each of the children described, we would be overlooking the fact that refusing to clean up had a different meaning for each. Instead, our choice of tactics should reflect the different meanings: perhaps a clear and timely warning for the first child, a "save" sign for the second, and planned ignoring for the third. Therefore, choosing tactics according to what problem behaviors mean to children is one way to solve the problem of the match.

To illustrate another way of matching tactics to children, consider the following examples: In one class, a sweet-looking toddler with very little speech frequently bit others. The teacher tried guidance, but it did not work. Nothing worked until she simply held the child's shoulders gently, just to get her attention, and said in a firm, but not angry voice, "No bite!" In another class, a slightly older and more verbal child also bit others. But here, initially, the teacher tried directives, but that tactic did not work. What worked was when the teacher switched to guidance tactics that helped the child use words rather than bite. In these two examples, the teachers succeeded only after they matched tactics to the children's respective developmental levels—what is often called "developmentally appropriate practice."

Matching Tactics to Circumstances

Like some Chinese entree, many children can be sweet most of the time but sour at other times, such as right before lunch. This is a simple example of how circumstances can inform us about what tactics to use on problem behavior (a cracker, perhaps, or something small on which to munch, for the child who is cranky before lunchtime). Another example of matching tactics to circumstances is the following: David, a troubled child, often engaged in tantrums, forcing teachers to hold him for long periods of time. To the teachers, there was nothing else to do. To them, they were following strict behavior modification rules: rewarding David when he behaved nicely, punishing or removing him when he behaved badly. But a closer inspection of immediate circumstances revealed a different story. Before David had his tantrums, teachers usually were telling him what not to do. By their own reports (and those of an independent observer as well), they were always doing so "in a reasonable way." If these teachers had attended to the circumstances surrounding David's tantrums, they might have seen that their being reasonable (or, rather, their sounding reasonable) was what set off the tantrums! This rather startling conclusion was supported by another observation. With one teacher, David almost never engaged in tantrums. Whenever David was about to do something he should not do, rather than sounding reasonable, she empathized, mirrored his feelings, and only then prevented him from going his own (unacceptable) way.

Matching tactics to circumstances can also mean matching to circumstances outside the classroom, especially to circumstances in a child's family. For example, it is important to use a softer approach to discipline with a child who has just lost his father to divorce than would be used with another misbehaving child whose family is intact. And we might appeal to the pride and satisfaction of being a big brother or sister to a misbehaving child with a new sibling.

Types of Tactics

To help teachers mix and match tactics, I have grouped tactics into three different types: *guidance, prevention,* and *control*. Table 2.1 lists examples of tactics grouped according to their type. Control is the aim of all three types of tactics, but as the category labels suggest, the first two have additional aims as well. Guidance tactics aim primarily at promoting inner resources and more mature behavior.

Table 2.1. Types of Tactics for Managing Behavior Problems by Type.

Guidance Tactics	Prevention Tactics	Control Tactics
Educational management	Distracting	Directives
Logical consequences	Intentional ignoring	Rules
Co-playing	Defensive grouping	Negative consequences
Paradoxical roles	Proximity control	Rewards
	Humor	Physical interventions
	Reframing	

Prevention tactics aim primarily at preventing behavior problems and unnecessary battles between teacher and child. Control tactics aim primarily at immediate control of children.

Guidance Tactics

Because their central role is to promote inner resources and more mature behavior, guidance tactics fit most comfortably within a developmental approach. Some guidance tactics start out as directives or negative consequences, then their true nature is revealed when teachers go on to guide. An example is when a teacher says "Don't hit; use words" and then goes on to suggest words and to see that the child practices using them. I call these kinds of guidance tactics educational management.

Some negative consequences may guide because they are logical (Dreikurs and Grey, 1990). An example of a logical consequence is making a child lose his or her turn in the block corner when the child refused to put away blocks the day before. My favorite example of a logical consequence is not from the classroom but from Laura Ingall Wilder's book *On the Banks of Plum Creek*. In this example, Laura has recently confessed to going near the creek, something Pa told her never to do. Always the child expert and loving disciplinarian, Pa responded to her confession:

> For a long time he did not say anything, and Laura waited. Laura could not see his face in the dark, but she leaned against his knee, and she could feel how strong and kind he was. "Well," he said at last, "I hardly know what to do, Laura. You see, I trusted you. It is hard to know what to do with a person you can't trust. But do you know what people have to do to anyone they can't trust?" "What?" Laura quavered. "They have to watch him," said Pa. "So I guess you must be watched. Your Ma will have to do it because I must work at Nelson's. So tomorrow you stay where Ma can watch you. You're not

to go out of her sight all day. If you have a good day, then we will let you try again to be a little girl we can trust" [Wilder, (1937) 1965, p. 33].

When using logical consequences as a tactic, some caution is necessary: with young children, for logical consequences to guide, the logic must be carefully taught, just as Pa taught Laura about the logic behind having to watch her. After all, logic is not children's strongest suit.

Not all guidance tactics have an obvious lesson. Co-play is such a tactic. Co-play occurs when a teacher becomes a child's partner in play, when, for a while, a teacher relinquishes the traditional role of teacher in order to play in ways that help. Co-play is a powerful guidance tactic. In co-play with a teacher, children may express their most difficult feelings and exhibit those behaviors that prevent them from connecting with others. Through co-play, teachers can help children become more adept at managing feelings, more skilled at playing constructively, and more capable of sharing control.

Another guidance tactic that has no obvious lesson is the assignment of paradoxical roles, roles that give children an opportunity to behave in ways opposite to their problems. For example, I once consulted on a case of a little boy whose impulsiveness led to accidents. To counter his impulsiveness, we made him the class "safety inspector" whose job it was to periodically inspect to see that toys were put away and that children were being careful. To our satisfaction (and amusement), this tactic worked. The tactic guided him to be less impulsive, more careful.

Prevention Tactics

Prevention tactics aim to prevent behavior problems from occurring in the first place or to prevent unnecessary battles between teacher and child. In using prevention tactics, we arrange circumstances so that children cannot cause trouble, or we let children be children by our choosing not to interfere. Here, the principal concern is to prevent bad side effects that often come from struggles for control: in the process of controlling children, we can make children resent us so deeply or think of themselves as being so bad that we end up winning battles but losing the war for self-control.

With very young children, the prevention tactic of distracting children can be effective because infants and toddlers are distractible. This tactic is less effective later on when children can maintain their focus. Intentional ignoring is another common prevention tactic. The reference here is not to planned, systematic ignoring used to extinguish misbehavior but rather to isolated instances of ignoring. The idea is to avoid doing battle over every little wrong, especially when the child, if ignored, will stop misbehaving on his or her own. Another prevention tactic, defensive grouping, is for teachers to assign seats, place themselves between children, or otherwise arrange children spatially to reduce the chances that they will be disruptive. Proximity control (Redl and Wineman (1965) involves getting close to a child who is about to misbehave. Proximity calms and supports, which is sometimes enough for children to be good on their own. Humor also can serve as a prevention tactic, especially when used on a child who is about to provoke another. For example, in a class of four year olds, one little girl tested the teacher by calling him a "poo-poo head" and "kucka face." The teacher prevented a battle by leaning close and saying with a grin, "Kiss me darling." She smiled in return and ran away.

The prevention tactic of reframing comes from family systems theory. With reframing, the teacher redefines a problem in a positive way. For example, at meeting time, a child jumped up suddenly and started to dance. The teacher turned to the group and said, "Michael really likes to dance." Everyone, including Michael, had expected a reprimand, but the teacher framed the dancing not as misbehaving but as Michael expressing a special interest. Without comment, Michael rejoined the group.

One final note about prevention tactics: the tactics listed here are normally used with particular children. However, there is a whole set of prevention tactics having to do with programming, the physical environment, and developing classrooms. These classroom tactics are the subject of Chapter 9.

Control Tactics

At certain moments, we need not concern ourselves with development. We need only concern ourselves with getting a child to clean up, sit down, speak in a quiet voice, or whatever. That is, at certain moments, we need control tactics to get children to behave right now. The most common types of control tactics are listed in Table 2.1.

Directives such as "Stop hitting," "Pick up your coats," and "Don't run!" control children by telling them what to do and what not to do. Rules also control by telling children what they can and cannot do. The advantages of using directives and rules are clear. They are fast and simple. We need only say what we want or refer to a rule. There is nothing fancy about these control tactics: no extended reasoning, no clinical interpretations.

So why not rely solely on directives and rules to manage? One answer is they do not always work. Directives and rules work best when we have established a climate of cooperation between children and ourselves, when they trust that we will direct them in their best interests as well as our own. And directives and rules work best when children know that, if necessary, we will follow up with more powerful controls.

Negative consequences (or the threat of negative consequences) are more powerful controls. Time-out is one example. Time-out often follows a failed directive or violation of some rule. In classrooms for young children, time-outs are usually brief, three to five minutes only, with the child sitting alone but in full view of all others in the classroom. Of all the tactics for managing behavior problems, negative consequences are the most likely to violate Redl and Wineman's (1965) law.

Rewards (or the promise of rewards) are also powerful controls. Used thoughtfully and systematically, they can tame even the wildest child. But since taming is not the same thing as supporting development, their use also may violate Redl and Wineman's law.

Of all the control tactics, physical interventions are the most controlling. Physical interventions are necessary when there is immediate danger or when matters have truly gotten out of hand. Usually, teachers hold a child to prevent further mischief. No one enjoys resorting to physical interventions—at least, no one should. Physical interventions are tactics of last resort. The reasons are clear: they disrupt the class and leave little room for children to exert self-control.

Summary

Outlined here are the main tactics for managing behavior problems of individual children. We need to learn to use them if we are to manage problems, much as we need to learn lines in a play if we are to act. But just as acting entails more than learning lines, so too managing behavior problems entails more than learning tactics.

Part Two

· ·

Developmental Tasks for the Child

A new life task presents a crisis whose outcome can be a successful graduation, or alternatively, an impairment of the life cycle, which will aggravate future crises.

Erik Erikson (1962, p. 254)

I n Part Two, we look at behavior problems as symptoms of children struggling to master one or more developmental tasks, particularly the following: finding security, developing a healthy sense of self, becoming a constructive player, and making good friends. Here, more than anywhere, we see how development can be a cure as children are helped to outgrow their behavior problems.

3

· ·

Feeling Connected in the Classroom

N ot long ago, I observed a group of toddlers in a cooperative
day-care center. These toddlers were like most toddlers. They
moved at that slow pace characteristic of toddlers, especially while
being dropped off on mornings when parents are late and in a hurry.
Like toddlers elsewhere, they had their own peculiar ways of relating (or not relating, as the case may be): they sometimes looked at
others as if those individuals were far, far away. And their play con-
sisted of repetitious gatherings of objects into heaps and so forth.
These toddlers, then, did not impress me with their pace, their way
of relating, or their play. But they did impress me with their obvious attachment to their teacher.

The toddlers' attachment was best illustrated at lunchtime,
when the teacher eased the children from their play by introducing
games that brought them all to the table at one time and at their
own slow pace. But then came the awkward moment when the children had to be helped with their lunch boxes, the kind with metal
latches that are nearly impossible for toddlers to open. Also, a few
had wide-mouth thermos bottles that were equally difficult to open.

The lunch routine I observed was on a day when the teacher was
assisted by three student volunteers from the neighboring college,
each friendly and eager to help. But the toddlers rejected them,
insisting that only the teacher could do the job. So, while the three

students sat back looking somewhat sad and confused, the teacher went from toddler to toddler opening lunch boxes and twisting lids on thermos bottles.

This example illustrates the point that young children find security in forming attachments to teachers. It is with care that I use the term *attachment* here to describe a relationship other than that between parent and child. Obviously, from the child's point of view, attachments to teachers are not as strong and needed as are those to parents, but they are needed nonetheless. Indeed, there are enough parallels between how young children relate to their parents and how they relate to their teachers to make the term *attachment* useful for describing what we hope for in classrooms. The toddlers in the example above showed their attachment to their teacher by restricting who could help them. There are other, even more important ways that young children show their attachments.

Imagine a mother with her one-year-old daughter in a park. Let us say that while we are watching, the mother sits on a bench, sometimes reading, sometimes watching her child. What would we see the infant doing? Most likely, we would see her wandering away, exploring the grass, flowers, or whatever. But that is not all. We would also see her turn from her wanderings to come closer to her mother, perhaps so close as to touch. What we would see, then, is an ebb and flow to the infant's movements, a going out and a coming back that maintain a balance between the need to explore and the need to feel attached. What we would see, then, is the infant treating her mother as a secure base from which to explore.

Now consider the following example: Heather and Marianne, two delightful four year olds, busied themselves making "cookies" from Playdoh. While pounding and shaping, they fantasized together about the party they were to give—who to ask, what to wear, and so on. Suddenly, without warning, Heather turned in her seat and yelled to her teacher, "We're making cookies!" The teacher nodded and in an approving voice responded, "Oh, you're making cookies." Heather seemed pleased by the response and turned to resume play with Marianne. Anyone familiar with early childhood classrooms will agree that incidents such as this are common; young children frequently "check in" and share what they are doing with teachers.

These two examples illustrate a kind of returning to base, a seeking out contact after a period of exploring. Heather immersed herself in play with Marianne, but at the same time she maintained her attachment to the teacher, as evidenced by her thinking of the teacher even when her back was turned. And just as the infant's return to the mother fueled the infant for another bout of exploring, so too Heather's checking in with the teacher fueled her for continuation of play with Marianne.

Attachments to teachers are also evident in the way preschoolers seek comfort when hurt, guidance when confused, and alliances when attacked—not all of the time, just those times when the slings and arrows of classroom life become too much. And, of course, attachments are evident in the occasional requests for physical affection: a hand to hold, a lap to sit on, a hug or two.

This balance, then, between embracing challenges and requesting help, between immersing oneself in play and checking in, between meeting conflicts alone and seeking alliances, and between needing and not needing physical contact defines preschoolers' healthy attachments to their teachers. The balance signifies that for preschoolers there is someone in the classroom framing their constructive activity and problem solving, someone providing a safe haven and secure base from which to explore and challenge, someone willing to be an ally.

Clearly, teachers need a degree of professional distance if they are to focus on groups and remain invested in teaching even as children come and go. I am not suggesting, then, that teachers become mothers or fathers to their pupils. But I am suggesting that teachers develop relationships with children that in some ways parallel the (healthy) parent-child relationship so that children feel secure and come to want to behave and be partners in the running of classrooms. As Katz (1988, p. 47) has noted, "It may be possible for young children to feel very attached to their teachers . . . without the teachers' responding at the same level of intensity."

Attachments and Children with Behavior Problems

The main point of this chapter is that children with behavior problems need help forming healthy attachments to teachers, and they need help finding secure bases from which to explore. Some children do not attach at all, especially isolated children, who spend a good deal of time watching others and wandering, but also aggressive, uncooperative children, who show little concern for what a teacher wants or thinks. Other children may maintain infantile attachments by demanding constant attention, physical proximity, and contact. Whatever the specifics, the lack of secure attachments with teachers means these children do not have an important motive for behaving themselves and an important support for calming themselves as they explore the classroom. The argument here is that attachments to teachers, not reinforcement or discipline, form the overall context and primary motivation for preschoolers to share control, follow rules, and get along with others. Therefore, addressing problems in the way some children attach or fail to attach is the first order of business when treating behavior problems.

Attention to a child's attachment patterns is not the usual starting point in response to behavior problems, at least not in my experience. When I am asked to consult, the consultation session typically begins with my listening to teachers describe a child's behavior and background. Invariably, I hear a good deal about problem behaviors (hitting, whining, not sharing, and so on) and a good deal about family background, but not much about attachments to teachers. What is missing in the descriptions and discussion is any substantive understanding of how the child sees teachers and feels about them. I do not hear teachers asking, "Does this child feel my presence, or am I just a large blob on the horizon?" or "Does this child see me as a helper, guide, source of comfort, and ally, or does he see me as someone who simply imposes, limits, and judges?"

There are two main reasons why teachers do not generally put children's attachments to them as the first order of business. The first reason is that the behaviors listed earlier (asking for help and checking in) are not seen as attachment behaviors. The second reason is that attachment is seen as something that just happens, like falling in love, not as something we make happen. Obviously, I take a more active view.

Fostering Attachments

If indeed attachments are crucial to treating behavior problems and if an active view of the attachment process is the correct view, then how do we foster attachments? The answer lies in cultivating each of the behaviors I have mentioned as behaviors indicating healthy, normal attachments between teachers and young children. Take checking in as an example. In my experience, many disruptive, uncooperative children do not check in enough, do not share with teachers what they are doing and accomplishing. It simply does not occur to them that teachers might be interested. To counteract this mistaken belief and to cultivate checking in, we can do more than simply reinforce infrequent moments of checking in. We can ask children to check in, to come get us when their projects are finished. We can make clear that we are interested. Fostering attachments, then, need not be complex or strenuous.

The same is true for behaviors that call upon teachers to be helpers, guides, and allies. Teachers can join even difficult children in problem solving, in promoting their agendas, and in protecting their rights. In doing so, they help win themselves the status of partner. Put another way, with difficult children who are anything but partners, teachers need to take an active role in showing that they as teachers can at least hold up their side of a partnership.

Attachments and Control

Underlying the powerful emotions surrounding attachments, we find, once again, the issue of control. But here, the issue is about controlling proximity and attention as well as controlling intention. As Greenberg and Speltz (1988) pointed out, some children become aggressive and coercive as a way to gain control over their care-givers' attention, presumably because they have never experienced having a predictable, available, and sensitive caregiver. In the fol-lowing example, we see such a child: Every day for the first half of the school year, this child disrupted his class by making noises at meeting time, by destroying others' property, by hitting others with-out being provoked. The only times he was not disruptive were when he had his teacher's undivided attention:

> Aaron is at the writing table sitting next to his teacher, Susan. There are three girls with him at the table. Susan has helped him get started on his idea for a haunted subway story. She brings him a book on machines and questions him about what he has begun to draw. For ten minutes her questions and comments come in an almost steady stream. It looks exhausting. Aaron answers, draws, and looks at the reference book. But when Nicholas walks over to the table and asks Susan a question, Aaron loses focus, begins to play with his marker, begins to make puffing sounds. He leans over another child's paper and tries to distract her. After a while, he tries to regain Susan's atten-tion by pretending to hit her on the shoulder. She ignores him until he returns to drawing, whereupon she praises him for working. A few minutes later, Susan's attention is again drawn to another child. This time, Aaron simply walks away.

Aaron lost all sense of control when he did not have his teacher's attention. And for the first few months, he needed her attention, not just when he was bad but also and especially when he was good. With time and his teacher's hard work, he too found other ways to feel in control.

Quality of Attachments

Toward the end of infancy, attachment figures do not have to be physically present to have influence on a child because they become internalized. That is, children begin to carry around inside themselves their relationships with mother, father, or whoever has been a significant other. If those inner relationships are good and predictable, then children will take with them everywhere a real source of strength. It may be the case that those preschoolers who are productive and happy even while playing alone are those with especially happy internalized attachment relationships.

But if inner relationships are neither good nor predictable, the opposite follows: a child will feel anxious, angry, or unhappy, even in the presence of those who care. It will be difficult for teachers to help such a child simply by managing his or her behavior problems. Rather, the child needs new and better attachments, as the following case illustrates:

Seth, age four, entered his Head Start class at midyear. His father was in prison, and his mother worked long hours. When not in school, Seth stayed with a babysitter. Unfortunately, this babysitter disliked Seth and directed all of her affection toward her own son.

In the classroom, Seth played by himself. He could be creative with dolls, blocks, and paints, but his play never lasted long, and it lacked joy. Furthermore, whenever other children approached Seth or made gestures of wishing to join him, they were rejected with a scowl or an angry "Go away!" At times, Seth interrupted what he was doing to disrupt or destroy others' play. With a slight smile, he might

spatter paint on a child's clothes or kick over a child's block construction. With teachers, Seth was equally impossible. He ignored
their requests and taunted them by running away. Seth seemed quite
independent, hardly a child wishing for an attachment.

But Seth's independence was only apparent, not real. Toward the
end of most mornings, he became upset. Like a caged animal, he
ran back and forth, and then settled into a large closet to cry for his
mother, perhaps in anticipation of being picked up by the rejecting
babysitter, but more likely out of frustration over not knowing when
he would next see his mother.

What does one do in cases such as this? Simply being tough does
not work. It may even make matters worse by making a child such
as Seth feel more insecure and alone. What Seth needed was someone with whom he could attach and find security. One teacher was
chosen, and with time and her patience she gave Seth the kind of
nurturing attention he needed. Without much disciplining, Seth
responded by ceasing his disruptive ways.

Obviously, not every case of treating a disruptive child as an
attachment problem will have such a happy and easy ending. But,
in the majority of cases, attending first to the fostering of attachments is helpful.

Other Types of Connections

Attachments help children feel connected and not alone—a feeling absolutely necessary for young children to function well. But
there are other ways young children can feel connected.

At the start of each school day, children must physically disconnect from parents and home in order to connect with teachers,
peers, and school. Most preschoolers find or are given ways to
accomplish this task. For example, each day when my older son and
I arrived at his preschool, his teachers shouted warmly, "Here's
Will!" Whether rain or shine, cold or hot, their greetings always

made him feel connected. And Will played his part in feeling connected. Like many preschoolers, he brought objects from home: an action figure, a new toy, or something he had built. For him, the objects connected home and school as teachers and peers inspected them, commented on them, admired them.

In addition, I played a part in helping Will feel connected to school. When Will was two years old and often when he was three, good-bye embraces were clings, not hugs, symptoms of his feeling unsure about connections to school. By four, the greetings of teachers, the objects he brought from home, and the attention he got from peers were enough to make him feel sure. But just to be certain he felt connected, I encouraged him to prolong his hugs by telling him they were my fuel for the day. His hugs became longer, but they were never clings. Once finished, the memory of them still lingered. Once finished, he asked, "How long will that last, Daddy?" and then he separated easily, more ready to begin his day. I too was more ready.

But beginnings of school days are not always so full of connections, especially for children with behavior problems. Some enter the classroom as if shot from cannons. They dart about leaving little time for greetings or hugs. Others wander in and continue to wander, as if half asleep. Still others cling. For these children, we need to work extra hard to provide connections for the start of the day.

Once the day begins, most classrooms are filled with supports for children to feel connected: welcome songs during morning meetings, show-and-tell sessions later on, friendship groups during free play, and special friends programs, to name just a few. That is, the curriculum, schedule, and make-up of the average early childhood classroom offer many supports for children to feel connected at school.

For some children, however, these supports are not enough. For them, severing connections from home in order to connect at school seems especially difficult. So we need to do much more for and with them. The following is an example of an extremely shy child who could not connect at school until she made use of her imagination:

> Four-year-old Nina rarely spoke at school though at home she spoke all the time. When she needed help, she gestured. When she played, she did so by herself or silently alongside her peers. Her refusal to speak seemed her way to remain unconnected.
>
> Without connections to those at school, Nina found another way to support her need to feel connected; she developed imaginary friends. There was timid Minnie and the more adventuresome Alice, and there was Dumbo. Eventually, these friends provided enough support to become a way for Nina to make real connections. For example, two months into the school year Nina perched on the tire swing with two other children. They had been asking a teacher for pushes when Nina suddenly tossed her hand in the air and said, "Here you go, Dumbo!" The other two looked puzzled until Nina continued, "Here are some more peanuts, Dumbo!" When the others caught on, they too began tossing "peanuts," which made Nina laugh. And once, when the class was going on a field trip, Nina said, "Minnie doesn't like field trips. But I think Alice will come."

By allowing, even supporting, this child's imaginary playmates, both the teachers and other children were helping her feel connected. And through feeling connected, she eventually felt secure enough to participate fully in the classroom community.

Summary

Persistent behavior problems can be symptoms of attachment problems and of not feeling connected. Problems of attachment or connection, then, extend beyond the home and into the teacher-child relationship and the classroom as a whole. So, to treat young children's behavior problems, we need, first, to foster attachments and help children find security in their connections to teachers and the class. Furthermore, these kinds of attachments and connections that are so critical in early childhood are not infantile attachments and connections based only on physical contact but rather more mature attachments and connections based mostly on understanding, shared interests, and partnerships.

4

Developing a Healthy Sense of Self

One day I asked Seth, the boy mentioned in Chapter 3 who cried for his mother at the end of each school day, what kind of animal he would like to be if he could be any animal. He replied, "A monster." I knew what he meant, but just to be sure I asked, "A cookie monster?" "No," he replied, "A biting monster." A little while later he looked at me anxiously and asked, "I'm good, aren't I?" Apparently, Seth was not so sure he was good. In fact, his choice of animal and his anxious look suggested he felt quite the opposite.

Feeling good about oneself is a common theme in discussions of children with behavior problems, so common, in fact, that one might assume that poor self-esteem is the root of all behavior problems. Indeed, children such as Seth who have been treated poorly often develop poor self-esteem ("If they don't love me, then maybe I'm unlovable."). As a result, they act according to their self-images rather than according to the images they would like to have.

Saying that a child has poor self-esteem suggests a degree of self-consciousness not common in the very young. For the very young, not having a sense of self may be more the issue. Thus, when I use the term *having a sense of self*, I actually am referring to two kinds of senses. The first is a sense of being an agent, someone who makes things happen, someone with direction. I call this first sense of self a "directed self." The second is a sense of being someone with thoughts and feelings, someone with an inner self not directly perceived by others but a self who can nevertheless be known and shared. The main theme in this chapter is that helping children develop these senses of themselves as being directed and as having inner thinking and feeling selves is important, often crucial, to helping them with their behavior problems.

Directed Self

The eyes of newborns are striking for how large they can become without focusing. They open and squint; they see without seeming to see. By two months of age, those same eyes most definitely focus, especially on others. By two months, then, we see a directed self in the way in which infants look out at the world. But at two months, infants will look without reaching, even in relation to objects they clearly want. At two months, then, the sense of self as directed is still quite limited.

By nine months of age, the picture has changed dramatically. Now we see directed selves in the way in which infants reach, crawl, and explore. Their whole selves, then, not just their eyes, are directed. To capture this wholeness, Margaret Mahler spoke of nine month olds as being "hatched" from the shell-like hold of their mothers' arms, where mother and child once seemed like one (Mahler, Pine, and Bergman, 1975). Using a different metaphor to capture the centrality of this sense of self, Stern (1985) referred to a "core" self emerging whole and directed.

The core, directed self of the hatched nine month old is not there all of the time, however. Sometimes, this sense of being a directed self gets lost, especially when children feel insecure, as in the following case: Miko was new to her class of three year olds. For the first two weeks, she wandered and whimpered and looked very sad. Teachers tried to console her, comfort her, remind her that her mother would return, but to no avail. Without her mother, Miko had lost the sense that she could take direction on her own. More than consoling, Miko needed help regaining her sense of being a directed self. Help came gradually and in simple ways, such as when one teacher helped her direct scissors to cut tracings. Also helpful were the times teachers engaged Miko in co-play, when Miko regained direction by giving teachers directions ("Miko, where should I put this block?" "Miko, should I use a blue marker or a yellow one?"). Eventually, Miko's directed self was evident everywhere: in her focused expression at meeting time, in the serious way she threw herself into projects, and in her active contributions to group play.

Miko's feelings of being lost and helpless were temporary. For other children, those feelings last much longer, as was the case with Margaret. Whenever the horse Margaret was drawing proved too big for the paper, whenever the details in her tracings seemed too fine for her scissors, whenever the popsicle sticks in her collage loosened after gluing, whenever anything big or small went wrong, Margaret had only one response, "I can't!" At first, there was no solution except for teachers to help Margaret. Gradually, however, as teachers responded more when things went right and less when they went wrong, when they got Margaret to think about the way she took direction, she changed: "How did you figure out which colors to choose, Margaret?" With this kind of positive attention and these kinds of affirming questions, Margaret began to maintain her sense of being a directed self in bad times as well as in good.

For most observers, Miko would not be considered a behavior problem, and, for many, Margaret might not either. But David most definitely would. David often disrupted meetings by rolling on the floor, swearing, and interrupting teachers with rude comments. When removed from meetings, he protested, "I can't help it. My mouth gets me into trouble. I wish I could cut it off." And when frustrated, he engaged in tantrums. For example, once while playing with Legos, he shouted, "That's not fair! He has two of those [flat green pieces] and I only have one!" Instead of finding ways to continue, David threw his pieces and walked away. David's teacher wisely saw his problem as one of direction. "You are the boss of your body," she reminded him after his removal from a meeting. "Show me how you can use these other pieces," she responded in the Legos incident.

Although David had problems, he also had strengths. When not frustrated, his work could be among the best. In contrast, Harold's work was never among the best, especially when with peers:

> Harold wandered into an enclosed area where Jason was pushing his train. As Harold wandered, he nudged a small section of track and smiled slyly. Jason screamed, "Harold! Stop that!" Harold responded by balancing his body precariously and threatening, "I'm gonna crash your train!" "Harold!" cried Jason. A while later, Harold watched two boys, Kailin and John, who were building a boat with big blocks. "We're hunting for sharks! We're gonna bomb them!" said Kailin. He and John made a pile of small blocks they called "bombs." "Now we need to bomb them," announced Kailin, whereupon he and John donned safety goggles and "swam" with their "bombs." But then Harold suddenly pushed the boat over. "What did you do that for?" Kailin said. "I don't know," Harold replied with a grin. "Well, you need to help us fix it," responded Kailin. "No I don't," said Harold as he walked away.

Harold's problem was that he never found a positive, directed self in social play with peers. While others made things happen by shouting instructions, making suggestions, asserting their ideas, Harold just watched, watched until finding direction in victimizing others seemed a better alternative than having no direction at all. Indeed, children such as Harold present major challenges to teachers because they need so much and because they make those around them so mad. It is hard to care for anyone who seems to enjoy others' pain.

Losing or not having a directed self, then, takes many forms: feeling lost, feeling incapable, feeling out of control, feeling victimized, feeling the need to victimize. Regardless of the form, when children do not have directed selves, the result can be behavior problems: aimless wandering, being too dependent, disowning misbehavior, tantrums, destroying others' work, to name just the few discussed here. Whatever the specific behavior problem, the solution is to find ways to restore or develop a child's positive sense of being a directed self.

Finally, with respect to supporting young children's directed selves, the point emphasized in Chapter 1 about sharing control needs to be made again here, but for a different reason. The will and direction of young children often run counter to the will and direction of adults. This is normal and, up to a point, good. This is the price we adults pay for supporting the development of directed selves. So, wise adults react to clashes of will with caution and care. Wise adults sense that too much, or too little, discipline and adult direction can undermine the development of directed selves. Too much can squash budding selves or make them unwilling to bend. Too little can let them grow and become like weeds dominating all that surrounds. The fostering of directed selves, then, is one goal to be balanced against many.

Thoughts, Feelings, and the Inner Self

Infants as young as two months show thoughtfulness in their gazes and a surprising range of feelings. But their expressions of thoughts and feelings hardly signal self-conscious awareness of thoughts and feelings. Such awareness of one's *inner* life is something gained, not given, gained over a long period of time and with a good deal of help.

At first, infants depend on others to reflect how they feel. A good example of this reflecting is the following: "A nine-month-old girl becomes very excited about a toy and reaches for it. As she grabs it, she lets out an exuberant 'aaah!' and looks at her mother. Her mother looks back, scrunches up her shoulders, and performs a terrific shimmy with her upper body, like a go-go dancer. The shimmy lasts only about as long as her daughter's 'aaah!' but is equally excited, joyful, and intense" (Stern, 1985, p.140).

In the classroom, such reflecting goes on all the time, though usually not with shimmies: "Yes, Donald, I see how you've built that car!" says one teacher to reflect a child's pride. "Oh, Mary, what a shame!" says another teacher to reflect a child's hurt at falling down. In the classroom, then, reflecting thoughts and feelings is as natural as it is in the home, except perhaps when it comes to children with behavior problems.

Children with behavior problems often make it harder for adults to reflect thoughts and feelings. Withdrawn children give us few thoughts and feelings to reflect. Disruptive children give us thoughts and feelings we do not want to reflect, at least not in the empathic way necessary for fostering their awareness of their thoughts and feelings. But children with behavior problems need reflecting even more than others because they, more than others, often lack a sense of how they think and feel.

Besides reflecting thoughts and feelings, teachers help young children develop a sense of their thoughts and feelings when they help children communicate their thoughts and feelings directly. With regard to behavior problems, this kind of communication is especially important in times of conflict: "That makes me mad," says Mary when someone teases her. "I don't want that story. It makes me too scared," says David when offered a choice at reading time.

For young children, communicating thoughts and feelings directly is difficult at any time, but especially difficult when they are feeling intensely. It is difficult for at least two reasons. First, talking about one's thoughts and feelings requires a keen sense that thoughts and feelings are centered within and make up an inner as opposed to an outer reality. But for young children the lines between inner and outer are often unclear. Second, with only a limited vocabulary and only a limited command of language, young children can easily lack the right words to express thoughts and feelings or choose words that miss the mark.

Because communicating thoughts and feelings is so difficult for young children, they need help. In the following example, the teacher's response to problem behavior illustrates that help as well as the tactic of educational management:

> David and Billy were in the block corner when David grabbed one of Billy's blocks. Billy let out a shriek and lunged for David. But before Billy reached his target, his teacher grabbed him. "Tell David how that makes you feel, Billy." Unable then to express his rage directly, he squirmed in his teacher's arms, his frustration mounting. But he managed to calm himself enough to say tearfully, "That makes me mad!" "Tell David what you want him to do." "Give it back!" said Billy, his composure now somewhat regained through his ability to talk about his anger. David did give up the stolen block, more it seemed because of the teacher's presence than because of Billy's words and feelings. But for Billy the motive did not matter.

What is added to the sense of having an inner life by communicating thoughts and feelings directly? First, putting thoughts and feelings into words gives children an understanding of their thoughts and feelings. Second, the expression of thoughts and feelings fosters self-control and thereby reduces the likelihood of children acting out. Third, communicating thoughts and feelings provides at least an opportunity for others to understand and become friends.

Adults sometimes try to edit a child's thoughts and feelings so that only parts of the self are experienced as acceptable. This editing does not help. In fact, it can contribute to a child's problems. For example, Mary, a five year old who had been without friends for over a year, was outside on the playground collecting pinecones. While handing one to a student teacher, Mary said, "This is poison." The student teacher asked her what the poison was for. In response, while pointing to the other children on the playground, Mary said, "For the bad guys." The student teacher responded by saying that no one on the playground was a bad guy, that everyone was good. Mary seemed displeased and ran off. Here was an opportunity for this little girl not only to own and integrate her negative thoughts and feelings by embedding them in play but also to connect to someone who mattered. But it was an opportunity missed because the student teacher did not accept the thoughts and feelings expressed in Mary's play.

The following example shows just the opposite. By supporting his fantasies, the teacher helped a child own and integrate parts of his inner self that had been troubling him:

John was a four year old who remained distant from teachers, ignored their requests, and kept children away by growling whenever they came close. He sometimes hit children without being provoked, and, occasionally, he hit himself.

Once, shortly after John and his teacher began building with blocks, he answered her question about what they were building by saying, "A house with an alligator." After a while, he announced, "The house is done; now the alligator wants supper." "What does he like for supper?" the teacher asked. "Well," he said, "he likes octopus and [leaning closer to the teacher] sometimes girls with yellow hair for dessert." The fact that John's sister had blonde hair made the meaning of this fantasy clear.

Over the course of the next two weeks, John's teacher elicited several other sister fantasies. For example, after drawing a picture of a house and after being asked to explain what the scene was about, John said that his sister lived under the house because, "We like to keep her there." In John's picture, he lived upstairs with his mother and father. On another occasion, while he and his teacher were building a windmill out of Construx, she asked, "Does anyone live in there?" He responded, "My sister," and then laughing loudly, "She's locked up." John went on to say that a fox lived in there too, eating all the mice. "The fox will jump through the window, but he'll be okay. He has a parachute. Then he'll live in the forest and eat mice. He doesn't like the windmill 'cause my sister's there."

What is remarkable here is that this sharing of his sister fantasies in co-play proved to be all that John needed. Very soon, he grew close to his teacher, sat on her lap at meeting time, and sought her out to share. More remarkably, he stopped growling and started to play with the other children.

5

. . . .

Becoming a Constructive Player

Play is a means of meeting three goals that must be met if young children are to thrive and develop: connection to others, distance between impulse and actions, and vivid and tolerable thoughts and feelings. If children have problems playing, they can become isolated and impulsive and fail to control their feelings—all conditions promoting behavior problems.

Play and Isolation

The following is an example of how problems playing can isolate a child:

Andrew was a difficult child, often uncooperative with teachers and aggressive with classmates. He wanted to fit in. He just did not know how. For example, one morning, two children, Tom and Cathy, pretended to be fish swimming near a beach. Andrew watched and then moved nearby, making loud roaring noises, which he explained was his way of being a shark. Tom and Cathy accepted this initiative and "swam" away.

The three repeated this scene until Tom became bored and suggested to Andrew, "You don't have to be an angry shark all the time. You could sometimes be angry and sometimes not." Cathy added, "Yeah, if you are nice to us, we'll be nice to you, and we won't run away." Andrew rejected the bait and stuck to his role as an angry shark. So, to keep the play moving but in a novel way, Tom and Cathy created a "rock" where fish could be safe from sharks. This puzzled Andrew. Not knowing what to do, he walked away.

Andrew was deficient in make-believe play, which depends on a child's ability to generate stories and play off the stories of others. The following is another example of how Andrew's problems in playing served to isolate him:

Andrew and Tom were playing alongside each other with animal figures. Eventually, Tom asked, "Do you want to play with me?" Andrew did not respond, so again Tom asked, not once but several times. Finally, after noticing one of the doll figures, Andrew replied, "Okay, I want to be the guy." Tom replied, "Okay, I'll be the animals." Andrew began moving the guy doll in and out of the animals while making silly, nonsensical sounds. Tom exclaimed, "Stop it, Andrew!" but Andrew did not stop. A teacher intervened to show Andrew how he might have the guy doll interact with the animal dolls. Tom took up this play, but Andrew continued to act silly in ways that failed to move the story along. The play was ruined.

The next example involves a boy whose problems playing were more basic and general than Andrew's, resulting in his being even more isolated than Andrew. No matter what the type of play, Raymond almost always found it hard to play off of others' play:

Two boys built a cozy house out of plastic blocks, all equipped with blankets and pillows. They established their roles as baby and father. "Put it right there, Dada," said Scott while pointing to the floor. "Okay," replied Bill, "Time to go to sleep, baby." Bill then pretended to tuck the baby in. At this point, Raymond entered the play as a ghost. At first, the others were excited by this addition. Bill yelled, "Cover your eyes, baby!" and while running away called, "Come scare me

ghosty!" Raymond ran after Bill and stole his blanket. Bill began to
cry, which led a teacher to intervene.

Later, while a teacher filled wading pools, the children skipped
from one pool to another, giggling and screaming. One girl, laughing,
approached Raymond and then ran away. Raymond ran after her and
tried to tickle her, which scared her so much that she started to cry.

Raymond's play never quite followed what the other children
were doing. In the first setting, he responded to the nurturing scene
by becoming an aggressive ghost. In the second, he responded to an
invitation to chase with unwanted tickling.

This inability of many children with behavior problems to play
off of others' play, especially others' make-believe play, has been well
documented in a research project that colleagues and I have been
conducting to study systematically the play of young children with
behavior problems. Part of that research involves asking children
to complete stories, with dolls, that are started by an examiner. In
one of those stories, the examiner has a giraffe doll play with animal friends. The giraffe doll then finds himself lost in the woods,
and the child's task is to play off of this scene and problem and continue the story to completion, presumably by having the giraffe
somehow find his way home. In the following example, a child
without behavior problems completes the story, playing off the
examiner's story stem and developing an effective resolution to the
problem of being lost: The child takes the giraffe doll and has the
giraffe ask each of the other animals, "Do you know the way to my
house?" Each says no. The last animal asked adds, "Why don't you
use your tall neck to see if you can see your house." The child then
has the giraffe look around and spot his house. The giraffe thanks
the animal who made the suggestion, and then he trots home.

In contrast to this story completion, consider the following
"completion" by a boy with obvious behavior problems. The child
grabs the giraffe and while knocking over each of the other animals
with it, he repeatedly says, "He's lost." After all the animals have

been knocked over, the child puts down the giraffe and turns to the observer to signal that he is finished. Here, the story completion is deficient because the child does not play off the story stem (no resolution of the problem) and the story is undeveloped. It also is arbitrarily aggressive. We are still in the process of completing this research, but so far the results indicate that, as a group, older preschoolers with behavior problems have an especially hard time developing narratives and collaborating in make-believe play.

Play and Impulsiveness

In the cases of Andrew and Raymond, deficiencies in play explain their broader problem of being isolated, of not connecting with their peers. But there are cases where the children connect but still have behavior problems. These are cases where the behavior problems derive from the inability of the children to use play to curb impulsiveness. Jerome was such a child. Jerome had friends, but because of his impulsiveness, his friendships were often stormy, and the storms often disrupted the entire class. For example,

> Jerome and three other boys busied themselves with big blocks. Together, they created a square-shaped structure with an opening in the middle, just big enough for them to stand. For awhile, Jerome lounged on top of the structure, then suddenly and without warning he stood and cried out, "Let's bomb the bad guys!" and he jumped. As he jumped, Jerome knocked over the top row of blocks. Warren screamed, "Now look what you've done! You've ruined our structure." Jerome responded angrily, "Shut up, stupid!" and then stormed off, teary-eyed, shoving blocks while he yelled, "Everybody's always picking on me!"

Jerome's play often was about his favorite superheroes, the Power Rangers. He and his friends would run around being Power Rangers until they were stopped by a teacher. When building with blocks, they usually made simple forts to keep themselves safe from the bad guys. And when the imaginary bad guys arrived, they were met with karate kicks and shots from pretend guns. Although this play might look age-appropriate (Jerome was almost six.), it was not. Foremost, the story lines never developed beyond kicking, punching, and shooting the bad guys. There were never any coordinated roles, developed plans for a new attack, or elaborate constructions to serve as props. In short, compared to others' play, Jerome's play, even when it was social, was underdeveloped and, being underdeveloped, could not serve as a wedge between his impulse to be aggressive and his actions.

This notion of play serving as a wedge between impulse and action is well illustrated by a simple, hypothetical example. Consider two boys, one who approaches us, points his finger, and says, "I'm going to shoot your eyes out," and the other who does the same thing but says, "I, Darth Vadar, am going to shoot your eyes out." My question is, which boy makes us feel more nervous, more anxious, that he might actually behave in an impulsive, destructive way?

When I ask this question (and I ask it a lot), almost everyone I ask answers that the first boy makes them more anxious, even though they do not know exactly why. In this case, intuition serves us well because, over twenty years ago, Rosalind Gould demonstrated that children who use the "direct I" when pretending are more likely to be disruptive than children who adopt a role, such as the role of Darth Vadar (Gould, 1972). It is ironic, then, that children who go deeper into their fantasy play by adopting roles and by developing elaborate stories are more apt to keep the boundaries between fantasy and reality both sharp and clear. This is a point often lost on adults who worry about children getting lost when developing their fantasies into stories.

Getting back to Jerome, I have one more observation to offer about his play not serving as a wedge between impulse and action. Some types of play stimulate impulsive, disorganized action more than do other types. Dramatic play is usually the most stimulating because it involves action from the start. In contrast, because it is a static medium, drawing is less likely to stimulate action. Drawing, then, can be an effective wedge between impulse and action. It is thus relevant that Jerome did not draw.

Having interpreted Jerome's inability to draw as his not having a tool to curb his impulsiveness, teachers began systematically helping Jerome draw Power Rangers fighting the bad guys. They modeled such drawings and prompted him to draw his own pictures. Further, they reserved a corner of the classroom where, for awhile, his pictures adorned the walls. For awhile, then, Jerome became the classroom's "artist in residence."

Jerome's drawings got better, and his behavior improved. We cannot be sure that the drawing contributed to his improved behavior, but over the years we have accumulated enough examples like this to become convinced that support of children's drawing and other forms of constructive play (block building, sculpting, and so on) helps to curb impulsiveness. On logical, not just empirical, grounds, this conclusion is not surprising. After all, a child cannot simultaneously be impulsive and construct something in organized play.

Making Feelings Both Vivid and Tolerable

Making thoughts and feelings both vivid and tolerable through play has been the traditional focus of therapists, so much so that some teachers shy away from helping children express thoughts and feelings in play: "It's not my role as teacher" and "I'm not a psychiatrist." I often hear these and similar statements of justification for not getting involved in helping children use play to make their thoughts and feelings vivid and tolerable.

Teachers who do not want to help children express their troublesome thoughts and feelings through play fail to realize that supporting children's play for this purpose need not be something fancy or clinical. Usually, there is no need for subtle interpretations. In classrooms, all that children really need is a way to express thoughts and feelings *in* their play.

By expressing thoughts and feelings in play—what I call "embedding thoughts and feelings" to emphasize the containment of feelings in play—children can control or manage their thoughts and feelings. In Chapter 4, I offered an example of a teacher helping a child (John) embed his jealous feelings toward his sister in play. That embedding led the child to bond with his teacher and to make friends with his classmates. In the following example, a teacher helped a child with behavior problems make his troublesome thoughts and feelings vivid and tolerable through embedding of his thoughts and feelings in play:

> Steven was loud, boisterous, and extremely aggressive with class-mates. He hit children without reason, threatened teachers, and was impossible during transitions. After three months on the Head Start bus, he was suspended for hitting, swearing, and shifting the gears of the bus. There was no great improvement until one day, in class, Steven drew a detailed picture that included flowers and a human fig-ure. His teacher patiently and skillfully got Steven to talk about his picture. Steven told her that the figure in the picture was his teacher, and that she had blood coming from her eyes. He went on to talk about death and burying people. As he talked, the teacher hid her feelings of shock and simply encouraged him to draw more and talk.

Not long before he drew this picture, Steven's grandmother had died. The picture may have been his attempt to overcome his con-fusion and feelings about her death. Whatever his motivation, the creation of that picture marked the beginning of an attachment to his teacher and a greater willingness to cooperate.

This example illustrates the importance of play as a way to embed troublesome thoughts and feelings. But it also illustrates how important it is for teachers to elicit and accept the fantasies behind children's play. The teacher in this example told me later that she would not have reacted to Steven's drawing in the manner that she did had she and I not talked prior to the incident. She would have tried to "clean up" the fantasy and make it "nice." Our conversation and the incident itself convinced her that through the embedding and sharing of thoughts and feelings children can gain control of difficult emotions. This is the same point that I made in Chapter 4 about the development of a healthy sense of self. I make it here once again but with an emphasis on the development of children's constructive play.

In another case of helping a child cope with difficult thoughts and feelings through the embedding of those thoughts and feelings in play, I was demonstrating to a student teacher how she might use co-play to help the child with her anger, sadness, and isolation. In this example, I played off the child's adoption of the role of an angry, put-upon mother not by encouraging her to be nice and nurturing but by encouraging her to go further with the role:

> Maggie, a tall and beautiful four year old, always came to school tired and angry. Throughout the day, she remained distant, removed, and somewhat sad. Her favorite play was to dress up in scarves and glide around the room, which was not unusual for a girl her age. But she glided as if in a trance, with none of the giggles that usually accompany such play, and she did nothing more organized than gliding. Furthermore, while she tolerated others, there was no one with whom she was close.
>
> Maggie came from an unhappy family, one in which the parents had serious marital problems. Occasionally, she gave teachers glimpses of her family. "Shut up!" she yelled when told to sit still. "Who says that?" asked a teacher. "My daddy," she responded. "Your daddy?" "Yes, because he hates my mommy." Later, she said, "I don't have covers." "No covers, Maggie?" "Daddy has them on my couch." Still later, she said, "My mommy says she's going to eat my hamster."

Usually, Maggie's play was without form or story. But on one occasion she showed the beginnings of adopting a role. On this occasion, with an angry, put-upon expression, she busied herself by the stove in the house corner. I entered the area and asked, "Can I come in?" "Yes, come in," she answered sternly. "Where shall I sit, in this chair or this?" I asked, while mirroring her stern tone. "Sit here," she commanded. "Good," I said, "This chair is bigger. Now what do I do in your house?" "Eat!" she directed in her angry, stern voice. The play continued with me becoming increasingly demanding, "I'm still hungry. What do I eat now?" Each time I repeated that I was hungry, she gave me something new with the same angry, put-upon look and voice. Two other children entered the house area and began to play. Maggie acted upset. She angrily picked up what the others had moved or dropped. I said, "These kids make a big mess. Such a mess, and you having to do all the cooking, feeding the baby, washing the clothes. How do you feel?" "I'm angry!" she said with a furrowed brow. The play then erupted into Maggie tossing food and utensils onto the floor. "This a big mess," she said, storming back and forth while dumping everything from the cupboards. "What is this play called?" I asked. "Is this 'angry mommy' play?" Maggie seemed pleased and continued to dump until everything was emptied. Before things got too out of control, I said, "That was good play, Maggie. How does this play end?" "We fix it," she said and then she proceeded to clean up her mess. I helped. "You did a lot of playing today, Maggie." "Yes, I be angry. You come back and play again?" "Yes," I replied.

On other days, the student teacher continued this co-play. To contain the mess, she and Maggie used a doll house. And there were variations. For example, Maggie and her student teacher developed a chanting game: "Maggie's got a doll," her teacher chanted while Maggie played. "I got da doll," Maggie sang. "Maggie calls her sweetie," chimed the teacher. "Sweetie, sweetie, sweetie," came the reply. "Now the baby's crying," the teacher said. "Bad, bad, bad!" Maggie scolded. "Now Maggie's mad," the teacher sang. "No, baby, no!" Maggie scolded. These sing-song games always ended in giggles, the teacher and Maggie now solid friends.

Happily, the friendship was not exclusive. Others joined in, and in a reasonably short time Maggie made a new friend with whom she spent most of her time in play.

Summary

Play can be an indispensable means for young children to develop in ways that run counter to behavior problems. Problems playing can isolate children and prevent them from using play to curb their impulsiveness and make troublesome thoughts and feelings tolerable. Moreover, deficiencies in play, particularly in make-believe and constructive play, can lead to behavior problems. In Chapter 6, I build on the discussion here because a child who cannot play, or cannot play well, is likely to be a child who has difficulty making friends.

6

Making Good Friends

W. George Scarlett and Jennifer Wickham

Not too long ago, a chapter on friendships in early childhood would have seemed strange because young children were assumed to be incapable of making friends. For example, in the early 1960s, Anna Freud (1963, p. 85) expressed the following opinion on the development of young children's outlook on peers: "[From] . . . a selfish, narcissistically oriented outlook on the object world, in which other children either do not figure at all or are perceived only in their role as disturbers of the mother-child relationship and rivals for the parent's love [to] . . . other children related to as lifeless objects, i.e., toys which can be handled, pushed arosund, sought out, and discarded as the mood demands, with no positive or negative response expected from them." Not much room for friendship here.

But toward the end of the 1960s and throughout the 1970s, research began to show the importance of peers to even very young children (Eckerman, Whatley, and Kutz, 1975; Lewis and Rosenblum, 1975; Mueller, 1972). It became clear that, given the opportunity to play with peers, children as young as eighteen months will develop preferred playmates whose parents and teachers usually describe as friends. But the question is whether having a playmate, even a preferred playmate, is the same as having a friend.

If we look at how young children explain their friendships, having a playmate and having a friend seem, for this age group, one and the same. "Jack and me are friends because we play together" is the most we can expect from a preschooler (Rubin, 1980). However, if we listen to what young children say when they are not around their friends and look at how they behave with their friends, then having a playmate and having a friend seem quite different.

Young children who have friends talk about their friends even when they are not around. That is, their friendships transcend momentary instances of playing together. Also, their talk uses the "me-and-___" construction for reference to themselves and their friends. The running together of "me" and the name of the other child symbolizes that the two are one. And the play of young friends is richer, more extended, more free-flowing than that of those who are merely playmates. These kinds of observations indicate that there are true friendships in early childhood, not for every child, but for a significant minority.

What does friendship in early childhood have to do with behavior problems? Our answer has three parts. First, the presence of a good friend can do much to undermine whatever it is that leads a child to misbehave. In particular, friendships demand sharing control, cultivating partnerships, and connecting with one another in satisfying ways, all of which create a context that runs counter to that which encourages children to misbehave. Second, at least a good percentage of those children who chronically misbehave are isolated children without friends. Being without friends, they become preoccupied with making mischief, perhaps as their only way to engage others. Third, there are bad friendships, friendships in which children become locked into patterns of relating that frustrate them to the point of fueling misbehavior. We return to this topic of bad friendships later in this chapter. First, we examine what young children need to do in order to develop friendships.

Negotiating Conflict and Sharing Experience

Chapter 5 provided ways to describe and evaluate peer play, focusing on whether children can "read" and play off of others' play. The discussion there also focused on how children structure or organize their play—as stories with characters and plots, as pictures representing actions and scenes, and so on. The aim was to provide ways to describe the foundation of young friendships, for young children do not make friends unless they play well. However, there is clearly more to being a friend than playing well, even in early childhood.

Robert Selman and his research colleagues have labored long and well to understand children's struggles to make friends in late childhood and adolescence, especially the struggles of emotionally disturbed children and adolescents. But though their focus is on older children and adolescents with serious emotional disturbance, their work can inform the way we look at young children in regular classrooms. As these researchers repeatedly have reminded us (for example, Selman and Hickey-Schultz, 1990), in order to make and keep friends, the task for everyone, whether young or old, troubled or carefree, is the same general task of balancing the aims of carrying out the self's agenda (satisfying needs for autonomy) and connecting with others (satisfying needs for intimacy). Selman and his associates have provided us with ways to show how children achieve (or fail to achieve) this balance. In particular, they have provided ways to evaluate how children of any age assert their autonomy through negotiation of interpersonal conflict and how children connect with one another through the sharing of experiences.

Selman's work sensitizes us to the fact that very young children (two year olds and many three year olds) do not even attempt to strike a balance. Rather, when faced with interpersonal conflict, they respond with naked power grabs or capitulations to avoid fights. Likewise, we are sensitized to the fact that very young children often share experience not so much through direct communication as through contagion. Two toddlers running up and down a hallway while squealing illustrate this point. Young children three to five years of age may not achieve the higher levels of negotiating conflict and sharing experience, but most go far beyond the level of toddlers.

In negotiating conflict with others, most preschoolers are able to give reasons to support their agendas and to refer to rules or procedures. However, in their negotiating, they may simply exchange agendas rather than work hard to coordinate them. In the following interaction, two three year olds (both friends) exchanged agendas as they discussed how to include toy dinosaurs in their play with blocks.

> SAMMY: (after placing two toy dinosaurs next to his block construction, which he called the "town") You're making a little town, right?
> WILL: Yeah.
> SAMMY: And I'm making a humongous town that belongs to these guys (pointing to the dinosaurs).
> WILL: Yeah, but one is mine, (*pause*) I don't know what I am making.
> SAMMY: You're making a town.
> WILL: No, I'm making a cave for my dinosaur.
> SAMMY: He's supposed to be in my town.
> WILL: Well, humongous giants have to live in a cave.
> SAMMY: No, they don't live in caves, dinos don't live in caves, they live nowhere, only on a straight path. Some dinos live on a turning path or a scribbly path. Some dinos live on a turning path. They only live on paths. That's where they live.
> WILL: But I'm telling you, I like to have my dinosaur in a cave.
> SAMMY: Well, sorry, your dinosaur wants to be in a humongous town.
> WILL: Humongous town is gonna make them cry.

This exchange was neither a fight, as evidenced by the calm, interested way in which both children continued the conversation, nor a coordinated effort to resolve a conflict. Rather, this was a pleasing negotiation over where the course of the fantasy should go. Will and Sammy simply exchanged ideas and then went their own ways in this make-believe play.

In the following example, two four year olds illustrate a slightly more advanced form of negotiating conflict. It is more advanced because the two eventually build on one another's ideas. In this interaction, Billy and Harold are playing with Sesame Street dolls. Harold has the Ernie doll driving a toy truck. A toy mailbox is off to one side. Billy has the Bert doll start to walk.

BILLY: Pretend Ernie gives Bert a ride in the truck.
HAROLD: No.
BILLY: Pretend the mailbox fell. (Billy tips the toy mailbox over onto Bert.)
HAROLD: Pretend somebody trapped Bert in the mailbox. (Speaking for Bert) "Aaagh! Get me out of here!" (Speaking for himself) Pretend he pushed the magic button. (Billy then responds to Harold's suggestion by pushing the "magic button," making Bert fly out of the mailbox.)

In the following example, from Selman and Hickey-Shultz (1990, p. 35), we see the most we can expect from young children in conflict negotiation. Here, Brian and Jeremy feel the force of arguments (reasons), even thought they focus on finding satisfaction for themselves alone:

When Brian arrived at Jeremy's house (Both children are six.), he quickly bursts through the door, threw off his coat, barely stopping to hang it up on an empty coat hook in the downstairs hall, and charged up the stairs with Jeremy in quick pursuit. They headed straight for his room. In the middle of the floor stood one of Jeremy's newest acquisitions, a latter-day "boys' doll house" recently handed down to him by his older brother, called the "Star Wars Death Star Space Station," modeled after the space station in the movie Star Wars. This highly visible toy was the immediate object of Brian's attention, and he headed directly for it.

As he did, Brian said, "Now, let's play a little bit here,"

referring to the space station model. His tone was firm and commanding. He quickly moved to the model, sat on the floor, and began to work the trash compactor, turning the knob that moved the wall in and out. At almost exactly the same time Brian made his move, perhaps a moment later, Jeremy, anticipating Brian's move, yelled out in a somewhat urgent tone, "I'm doing the trash compactor, Brian!" Jeremy then reached for the compactor knob as he spoke, but his hand arrived at the knob a moment after his friend's. Jeremy's look was questioning, both uncertain and concerned. Brian said with a slight scowl, "You've already played with this, but it's new to me." His tone was more forceful than Jeremy's, perhaps strengthened by the force of his argument, but it did not communicate anger. As Brian said this, he visibly tightened his grip on the compactor knob. Jeremy appeared to sit back on his heels for a moment, then drew back his outstretched arm.

Jeremy made no active challenge to Brian's assertion and claim, but showed his discontent by withdrawing from the joint involvement, moving away to the other side of the room. There he rummaged through a cardboard box of characters from the movie to play with. He carried a few of them to the floor and fiddled with them somewhat absently with a slight frown. Several seconds later he said aloud, "Okay, but next time I get to choose first!" Jeremy's statement was uttered in a matter-of-fact tone of voice; he apparently assumed it would be accepted with the same force of logic by Brian as Brian's statement was accepted by him. In any event, for whatever reason, Jeremy did not even turn around to check Brian's reaction. Indeed, Brian did take Jeremy's last "equalizer" remark in silence [Selman and Hickey-Schultz, 1990, p. 35].

As for sharing experience, young children may only rarely reach that level of sharing where individuals actively question one another so as to understand deeply. Nor are they likely to demonstrate as much interest in understanding another's experience as in communicating their own. However, most young children develop at least a rudimentary ability to communicate experience and at least a degree of interest in comparing experience. Selman and Hickey-Shultz (1990, p. 109) provide an example of such sharing with the following conversation between two (immature) eight year olds. As Selman and Hickey-Shultz noted, this conversation is marked by the girls exhibiting "kindred reactions" rather than genuine interest in one another, a kind of parallel play with words.

KATY: Do you know what I have? Surf and Tub. [She smiled as she named the toy.]
DENIA: I have this. [She pointed at something in the Barbie catalogue.] This kind, I have these kinds, and the pool.
KATY: I like the Surf and Tub. It's really neato. It has flipper. It has a mask thing. It even comes with its own separate tub. It's for California Barbie.
DENIA: Oh, that's nice. I have the ice cream one too.
KATY: My sister does.
DENIA: [rubbing stomach] Mmmm, I love ice cream.
KATY: I have Barbie News. I have Barbie Kitchen.
DENIA: I have, yeah, me too.
KATY: I have Barbie McDonald's.
DENIA: [showing Katy a catalog] I have this, see. . . . I have it. And I have a pony.
KATY: I have. . . .
DENIA: And I have this one. And I have the rockers, too.
KATY: [as both looked at the catalog] Let's see, I have this one.
DENIA: I have her. I have her, and I have the . . . I have her. I have lots of cars.
KATIE: I have cars.

DENIA: I have, I have a bed and her. And I have a house.

KATIE: I have, I have, Linda has this one.

DENIA: I have the house, too, and a bed. Ohhh, they're kind of pretty, all those Barbies. I wish I could have them all.

Exhibited levels of negotiating interpersonal conflict and levels of sharing experience provide important ways to evaluate both young friendships and the problems arising in young friendships. But, according to Selman and his colleagues, there is yet another way: to consider the "interpersonal orientation" of each partner, that is, the degree to which each partner is into changing the other or into changing themselves to make the friendship work. Most young children orient in both ways. Furthermore, most prefer partners who will work to change and be changed, making equality among friends the norm for young children. This issue of change is the same as that discussed earlier in terms of sharing control.

Some young children are consistent in their orientation. Either they insist on being the boss, on keeping all of the control and on having the other change, or they insist on following, on being controlled and on changing themselves to accommodate the other. If they can find a partner of opposite orientation and if they can find continued satisfaction in being in an unbalanced friendship, these children may not have problems. But, in most cases, these children do have a problem making or keeping friends. Furthermore, this problem of making friends can lead to behavior problems. Thus, we examine next how a rigid adherence to only one interpersonal orientation can prevent children from making friends and how it can promote behavior problems.

Interpersonal Orientation and Problems Making Friends

Many socially isolated children have problems making friends either because they will only be led or because they will only lead. Let us look, first, at those who will only be led and who also spend a good deal of time wandering and watching.

Wanderers and Watchers

In most classrooms of young children, there may be one or two who stand out because they almost never interact with others and because they spend a good deal of time wandering around the room watching others. These children often puzzle teachers both because they seem to have the skills to interact and because it is not clear what to do to help them.

For two years, one us (Scarlett) did his own wandering and watching by following socially isolated children around in their classrooms, videotaping them in large and small groups, and comparing their behavior to that of their classmates (Scarlett, 1980). The main research question was, What are these children doing to actively maintain their isolation?

The results of this study confirmed the obvious: by not playing much (because they were watching and wandering), these children made themselves unavailable for interaction. But the study also clarified the not so obvious, that is, the ways in which these children turned other children off when they did interact. It was not that they rejected others. They did not. It was that they never tried to change or control others, never suggested ways others might play. In short, they never were other-transforming. Rather, these were children waiting around to be led. The problem is that in most classrooms the vast majority of children want an equal as a partner, not someone who wants only to be led. Ironically, when teachers did try to help these children, they often did so by leading them—just what the children wanted but did not need.

As a follow-up to this first study, one us (Scarlett) began an informal study of a different approach, using co-play between teacher and child to get socially isolated children to lead (Scarlett, 1986). In implementing co-play, teachers first play in parallel and then begin to follow the children by imitating how they play. Then teachers actively request help, guidance, and suggestions from the children. That is, they lure the children into controlling them. Once a child gets into directing a teacher, showing the teacher how to play, and once this directing seems satisfying to the child, the teacher can allow other children to join in. This is not difficult since a teacher's play with one child usually attracts the attention and interest of other children. So, for a while, there may be threesomes, with the teacher still co-playing but in such a way that he or she can gradually withdraw, leaving the formerly isolated child to playing with another. Over the past ten years, many teachers have tried this technique for helping watchers and wanderers. In most cases, it has worked.

Used in this way, the teacher-child co-playing serves as a bridge between a child playing alone and a child playing with another. Furthermore, it serves to elicit just those behaviors that a child needs to practice if he or she is to make friends. Here, the behaviors all have to do with being other-transforming, that it, with leading and controlling another child.

Bossy Children

Bossiness is the everyday term for rigid adherence to an other-transforming interpersonal orientation and for insistence on keeping all of the control. Because they are so aggressive at seeking out others, many bossy children develop playmates. But many cannot keep playmates long enough for them to become friends. Here is an example of such a child:

Susie, age five, was a bossy child. Whenever she played with other children, she had to direct and control them, to the point where they would object and eventually leave the scene. For example, one day Susie and Tina were playing together. Susie said, "Let's play Care Bears (television characters). I'll be Tender Heart Bear. She's the prettiest." Then, from a crouched position, Susie said, "Look, I'm nice and soft and small like Tender Heart." Tina also became a bear, but she remained in a standing position. Susie told her that this was all wrong. "No, Tina, you can't stand up. Squish down, be small." Tina replied, "I want to be a big, tall Care Bear." Susie, losing patience, yelled, "There is no such thing. Now squish down right now!" Tina refused, whereupon Susie jumped up and started to push down on Tina's shoulders while screaming, "I said to squish!" This hurt Tina enough to make her cry. The play was ruined.

To help Susie become less bossy, one of her teachers began co-playing with her—at first by following Susie's lead (to establish rapport) but then by playing as an equal and occasionally insisting that Susie follow her (the teacher's) suggestions about how the play should develop. Here is a description of a play sequence in the first (following) stage of co-playing:

Susie sat by the playhouse. The teacher went over to her and said, "Hmm, this looks interesting. Could I play this with you?" Susie was delighted. "Sure, let me pick a person for you, and here is one for me. Okay, okay, now you make yours sick." The teacher responded, "I'll make my person cough." "No, no," said Susie, "Make her throw up, like this (she demonstrates). Okay, now I'll drive her to the hospital. Okay, lie yours here (the teacher puts her toy figure down). The doctor says you ate too much. That's why you're sick."

The teacher had been passive throughout, not being allowed by Susie to be active. Finally, the teacher has her toy figure say, "I'm feeling better now. I'm ready to go home." Susie was not pleased by this initiation and said, "Not so soon, young lady. You ate too much junk. Just lie down. I have a shot for you." The play sequence continued with Susie remaining boss and in control.

After establishing rapport, the teacher began a subsequent co-playing session: "Susie, let's play with these cars and the garage." Susie responded, "I want to play with you, but with the Legos." "Well, I'm playing with the garage now," said the teacher, "We can use the Legos another time." Susie folded her arms and said sternly, "No, I'm wanting the Legos now." The teacher proceeded to set up a few things around the garage. Slowly, Susie inched her way over. The teacher began to play, "I'm pushing a police car with a woman in it." Susie whined, " I want the police car with the lady in it." She grabbed for it, but the teacher intervened, "No, I'm using this now, you'll have to choose another one." "I want YOU to pick another one," said Susie. To which the teacher replied, "I had this one first, and I want to keep using it. When I'm done, I'll give you a chance." Susie started to look around. She found another figure. "I'm using her. She's even better."

After several of these co-playing sessions in which Susie and her teacher argued over who was to control the play, the co-playing began to have fewer arguments and became more like normal play. Susie seemed to be slowly giving up on trying to control so much. Here is an example:

Susie and her teacher were playing with matchbox cars. Pointing to the cars, Susie suggested, "Let's pretend they are police." Her teacher responded, "That's a good idea." Then taking another car, the teacher said, "Let's pretend this guy was speeding, and we go to catch him." "No, no," said Susie, "Let's make them go after that person because they got into a terrible accident." The teacher then suggested, "How about if we use both ideas? Let's pretend he was speeding and then got into an accident." "Okay," Susie agreed, "If I get to save him." She then proceeded to make the car speed and flip over. Her teacher said, "I like using both our ideas." Susie said that she liked using just her own ideas better. Then the teacher explained to Susie that she had more fun playing with her when they could use both of their ideas. To this, Susie responded, "At least you don't get mad and leave."

This last remark was a turning point. In subsequent co-playing sessions, Susie's teacher reminded her of the remark, to underscore the insight and make it really "stick." Susie began to see the connection between giving in a little and making friends. Co-play with her teachers showed her that she could find satisfaction even when not being the boss.

Thus, co-playing between teacher and child is not simply a matter of just playing. It is a matter of cultivating exactly those behaviors and the interpersonal orientation missing in a child's repertoire so that the child becomes better able to make friends. This goal is not always easy or simple to reach, of course. Sometimes, a single tactic such as co-playing does not work. Sometimes, the problems children have making friends are deep and the solutions called for are many.

In the following, final section of this chapter, one of us (Wickham) provides a summary of her observations of two children over the course of almost an entire school year. This case study clarifies how an unbalanced friendship, one in which one partner is the boss and the other is mostly a follower, can cause problems within the friendship and fuel behavior problems as well.

Bad Friendships and Behavior Problems: A Case Study

On my first day of observing in a classroom composed of kindergartners and first graders, my eyes were drawn to two boys playing in the block area. Paul and Alex were loud, aggressive, and reckless. They threw Legos, performed acrobatics, and yelled. They were friends, or so it seemed. They listened to each other, followed each other, and seemed to enjoy each other's company. For example, on one occasion Paul held up something he had made with Legos and said, "Da da da, now I've got him! Pretend Robin is really dead now." Alex replied, "Yeah! Pretend he stole it and knocked him into the river!" "Yeah!" agreed Paul, and he added, "Pretend he pushed him to the death, but he wasn't really dead, okay?" "Yeah!" said Alex passionately.

Though they were playmates, and possibly friends, Paul and Alex were quite different from each other. Paul was lanky, blond-haired, and handsome, despite having a disheveled appearance. Most of the time, he glided through the classroom with a quiet and knowing air, as if he owned the place. When not with Alex, Paul usually remained alone and aloof, content in his solitude, seemingly uninterested in playing with his classmates. Indeed, on his first day, Paul announced, "I will play with teachers. I don't play with kids." In contrast, Alex was red-haired and stocky. He looked the part of a class bully, but actually he was solicitous and eager to please. When not with Paul, Alex wandered or played with children, though never so intensely as when he was with Paul.

From the beginning of the school year, Paul was the one who caused trouble. On the first day of school, while the head teacher Merriam spoke during morning meeting, Paul interrupted and began to talk. He continued talking even after Merriam reminded him to listen while she spoke. Eventually, she was forced to say simply, "Stop!" whereupon Paul stood up and yelled. Again, Merriam told Paul to stop, this time in a louder voice. Stop, he did, but one sensed there was much more to come.

More did come. For the next few weeks, Paul continued to disrupt meetings. And outside of meetings, he engaged in tantrums. During the next month, with help from teachers, those tantrums stopped, but more subtle disruptions took their place. Quietly, Paul knocked down children's blocks, took their tools, touched (sometimes kissed) them against their will, and poured water into their sand table. As a result, most of the children began to stay clear of Paul. Alex was an exception. Alex was drawn to Paul. Each morning, he waited eagerly for Paul and showered him with invitations to play.

After a while, Paul's disruptiveness seemed to spread to Alex. At morning meetings, Alex began to giggle, make faces, and interrupt teachers. The situation got so bad that eventually Alex had to be removed. Furthermore, once removed, someone had to stay with and occupy him because if left alone, Alex threw things.

As I continued to observe, it struck me as significant that these two very disruptive children were friends. I had always thought of friendship as therapeutic, the kind of relationship that helps children learn to share control, cope with feelings, and engage themselves in meaningful ways. But, in the case of Paul and Alex, the opposite seemed to be true. It seemed that this friendship had a darker side that fueled, if not caused, the disruptiveness. For example, one morning, after about ten minutes of successful play, Paul took a game from the shelf and as he set it up, he explained the rules to Alex, who listened quietly. When the instructions were over and Alex began his turn, he asked Paul, "If I do it like this, is that okay?" Paul replied, "If you do it like that, you're never going to play with me again." To this, Alex said, "I won't Paul, don't worry." Paul's ultimatum seemed extreme to me and different from the usual five-year-old's hyperbole. Alex had asked a simple question about the rules of the game, and this resulted in his "friend" threatening to disown him. I wondered if this sort of thing happened often, whether Paul often forced Alex to do his bidding by threatening to dissolve the friendship. I also wondered about Paul's cool, sometimes rejecting responses to Alex's initiatives, such as the following:

Upon arriving in the morning, Paul went directly to the bulletin board to choose an activity. Alex approached him and said in his usual friendly way, "Hi Paul!" Paul ignored Alex, made a disgusted face, and walked away. He chose blocks, an activity with no other child present. After a minute, Alex joined him and said, "Paul! Whatcha' making?" Paul continued to ignore him. "Huh? Huh? Can I try?" pursued Alex. Paul nodded slightly, and Alex joined him. After a while and looking very much like the friends I knew from my initial observations, Paul and Alex busied themselves in their usual superhero play.

It was not surprising to me when Alex began to show frustration. Here is an example:

> Paul and Alex were playing with blocks, building their own, separate structures. Suddenly Alex exclaimed, "Why don't you want to play with me? I won't talk about that stuff anymore. I didn't anyway." Paul responded, "Yes, you did, right in the middle of it." Alex replied, "I promise I won't. It was a mistake. PLEASE! Please, please, please, Paul!" Paul got up, left the block area, and joined a group of children just settling down to a board game. Alex approached the assistant teacher organizing the game and complained, "Every time I play something Paul wants to play, he doesn't want to anymore." The assistant replied, "This is Paul's new choice. You can choose it too." Alex declined and remained on the sidelines to watch.

As Alex's frustration with Paul grew, he became an even greater behavior problem. He continued to have rough times during group meetings, but the out-of-control silliness (cracking jokes, making slurping and farting noises, and saying nonsense rhymes and then laughing hysterically) carried over through the rest of the day. During project times, Alex traveled around to different work groups, doing his best to get children to laugh at his antics. Usually, he succeeded.

Paul continued to test the limits of the room in quiet but very disruptive ways, such as by not cleaning up and by walking away from morning meeting. He also could be quite mean. Once, he grabbed another child's crotch when he thought no one was looking. And, once, without provocation, he threw sand in a child's face. But unlike Alex, Paul's problems seemed his own and not related to his friendship with Alex.

Toward mid October, the friendship took a turn for the worse as Alex started to rebel. Here is an example from that period:

Another child, Heidi, and Paul were playing well together in the block area with ramps and chutes designed for marbles. After about ten minutes, Alex wandered over and watched in an eager but hesitant way. When Paul saw him, he said to Heidi, "If you let Alex play, I'm not gonna." Alex mumbled something and Paul replied, "Yes, you did it last time. Well, Alex, you'll just have to work on it." Alex sat down quietly and began to build something. After about ten seconds, he picked up a big block, looked at Paul defiantly, threw it down hard on Paul's project (which had fallen to pieces anyway), and left the space. Paul glanced at Alex in a blank way and resumed his play.

And on another day, Alex was chosen to be "author" of the day and was waiting on the designated stool for his classmates to settle down. He was giggling and talking in a silly, affected voice when Paul walked by, put his hand over Alex's mouth and said in a stern voice, "I'm telling you now to be quiet. I don't like this." Alex, looking a little nervous, replied, "You're not the teacher. Remember, you're not the boss, Paul. Remember that."

Also by mid October, Alex could last for only about five minutes in morning meeting. His interruptions made it impossible for teachers to get anything accomplished. At the same time, Paul and two others were having difficulties as well, making meeting times frustrating for all. The teachers decided then that keeping these four children at group meetings was neither fair nor helpful to others. They decided to hold a separate meeting for those four until they could show enough self-control to rejoin their peers.

Merriam took over the small group while an assistant handled the rest of the children. The goals for the small group were turn taking, listening to others, and respecting others' points of view. When the children began to function without interrupting, Merriam began to read them stories. At the beginning and throughout, Merriam made clear to the children that they could return to the big group as soon as the goals of the small group were achieved.

Outside of meetings, teachers began to focus on giving Alex extra attention designed to foster closer attachments between Alex and them. The idea was to cultivate relationships that would give Alex the security he was searching for but not finding in his relationship with Paul. One assistant spent extra time with Alex and played with him, usually with cards since card games were Alex's favorite activity. More important, Merriam began taking Alex out of the room to tutor him on his writing. It was clear that he loved this added attention and perceived it as a privilege. The result of this special time was that, in Merriam's words, Alex "fell in love" with her. According to Merriam, he would beam when he saw her, gravitate toward her, show her his projects, and visibly bathe in her attention and approval. It was clear that he was increasingly willing to share himself with her. Although his time with the assistant provided Alex with companionship, the intensity of his feelings for Merriam overshadowed it. And though this is not what the teachers had planned, they were pleased to see Alex make his first, healthy friendship.

All of this happened at the end of December and the beginning of January. By mid March, the teachers reported a marked difference in Alex's ability to form friendships with a wider variety of peers. Although he would still spend time with Paul, his attention was not riveted on him. During that time, when I came to watch him, he typically was involved in some group activity, usually a card or board game. When assigned to a particular group for an activity, he involved himself with the children around him rather than scan the room for Paul, as he had done in the fall.

The teachers also provided Alex with curriculum activities more geared to his interests (music and movement). They helped him to get caught up in the material and to involve himself in work rather than in being disruptive. Alex now seemed proud of his achievements, able to feel good about himself through his work and not just through acceptance by his peers. Perhaps the strength he gathered from his connection to Merriam gave him the confidence needed to engross himself in classroom projects. Apparently, his need for connections was being met, and he no longer had to spend his time searching for ways to get inappropriate or unhealthy attention from others in the class.

By April, Alex had returned to morning meetings and remained without regressing. On occasion, he could be disruptive, but at such times he reacted to reminders from Merriam, reminders he used to ignore.

Although it is difficult to pinpoint exactly why Alex improved, it is clear that the tactics used by the teachers worked well enough to get Alex out of his role of Paul's compliant victim. He succeeded in several areas (learning to read, gaining Merriam's friendship, making new connections with peers, and being proud of his products), which gave him a new sense of pride and a new confidence in his ability to be an effective member of the class. Toward the end of the year, Alex drew a picture and wrote a brief story (see Figure 6.1) indicating that he understood that his relationship with Paul was not doing him much good.

Me and my friend aren't friends anymore.
I like it even though he is not my friend
anymore. The end.

Figure 6.1. Alex's Picture and Story About His Relationship with Paul.

Part Three

. . . .

Developing Classrooms

It is not the will or desire of any one person which establishes order but the moving spirit of the whole group. The control is social, but individuals are parts of a community, not outside of it. . . . [The teacher's authority] is not a manifestation of merely personal will; . . . [the teacher] exercises it as the representative and agent of the interests of the group as a whole.

John Dewey (1963, p. 54)

In Part Three, our lens widens as the unit of analysis switches from the individual child to the entire classroom. The main point here is that developing classrooms provides an excellent way to both manage and prevent behavior problems as well as a way to support children's development. We look at the task of developing classrooms in three related ways. The first way is developing classrooms into just and caring communities where individuals are motivated to share control as they come to identify with the group. The second way is developing curriculum to give children a voice that will secure for them a place in the community. The third way is developing thoughtful programming and arrangements of the physical environment so as to prevent or minimize behavior problems.

7

Building a Just and Caring Community

Lawrence Kohlberg and Thomas Lickona

The following is an excerpt of an essay from DeVries and Kohlberg's (1990) influential text on constructivist, developmental education. This chapter bears directly on our subject of a developmental approach to behavior problems by describing yet another way to develop classrooms as places where behavior problems are either prevented or managed in ways that promote development. This way is to instill throughout the classroom a sense of fairness and caring that is a step up from the very egocentric understandings of fairness and caring that are often associated with early childhood. In Kohlberg and Lickona's words, it is a way that works to "put morality on the inside."

One of my experiences a few years ago illustrates this problem of putting morality on the inside. While observing an early childhood special education program, I had the opportunity to join two boys and a girl for a snack. The snack of the day was cookies, and the rule was no more than two cookies per child. As is my custom when I visit classrooms, I found a way to test the meaning of classroom rules for the children by announcing that I was going to break the rule and have three cookies. I wanted to know which children had put this rule "on the inside."

The boy nearest me hardly looked up. His reaction to my breaking the rule suggested that, for him, rules come from the outside and are really no different from an adult telling children what to do.

The second boy looked surprised and puzzled, but then, with a shrug, he seemed to be saying I could do whatever I wanted. His behavior suggested that for a moment, at least, he was poised between two worlds: the world where those in authority rule and the world where rules govern everyone. He, then, was only just beginning to put morality on the inside.

In contrast to the boys, the girl was visibly annoyed, and after a brief pause, she announced with some irritation, "No, you can only have two." For her, my being an adult made no difference: a rule is a rule. Her morality, then, was definitely on the inside.

This example illustrates what is meant by putting morality on the inside, but it also illustrates the significance of this concept to the study and understanding of behavior problems. Specifically, my informal test of what rules meant to the children perfectly discriminated who was having the greatest difficulties around behavior problems. The first boy was having a particularly difficult time as he regularly was uncooperative and disruptive, the second boy had trouble occasionally, and the girl was really quite well behaved. As this example illustrates and as Kohlberg and Lickona explain in detail, morality on the inside does a better job regulating behavior than does morality on the outside.

W. George Scarlett

The research on moral reasoning in early childhood points consistently to this conclusion: Young children have a spontaneous tendency to view rules as the constraints that big people impose on little people. Might makes right. Asked why children should obey their parents, for example, one four year old replied, "Because children are the slaves of parents. We have to follow your orders."

As all parents and teachers know, however, the same four year old who sincerely asserts the absolute right of adults to be the boss nevertheless fails to follow adults' rules much of the time. How do we make sense out of this inconsistency between judgment and action? One answer is that for the child who equates morality with obedience to the arbitrary decisions of adults, rules have no inner logic, no felt necessity, no perceived practical purpose in social relations, and hence no real grip on behavior. Morality is not yet "on the inside."

The way to get morality on the inside is not simply to try to put it there. Straightforward didactic moral instruction certainly has a place in the education of the child, just as direct advocacy of justice has a place in the moral education of adolescents. But telling is not enough. Children must simultaneously *construct* or invent their moral understandings, much as they construct logical understandings like conservation, from the raw material of their firsthand experience. In the domain of social-moral development, that raw material consists of their day-to-day interactions.

Challenging children to think about the rules that should govern the social life of the classroom is a basic way to stimulate their construction of moral knowledge. A teacher can pose questions such as the following: What is a rule? Why do we have rules? Who should make the rules in a classroom? Why? Should teachers have to follow the same rules as children? Why? What rules do we need in our classroom? Why? What should happen if a person breaks a rule? Can rules be changed once you make them? How do you decide whether a rule should be changed?

Most teachers find that even before discussing rules for the classroom, they need to elicit rules for "good talking and good listening" in a discussion. Without such agreed-on rules, attempts to discuss any topic are often frustrated by egocentric behaviors such as talking when someone else is speaking, being silly, and getting up and walking around.

Some teachers prefer to let chaos reign temporarily in order to allow children to experience the need for rules of discussion. This is what Gloria Norton, a kindergarten teacher, did. She began her first class meeting with a discussion of the word *cooperation*, introduced by reading the fable of the chicken and the wheat. She and the children then discussed the book, naming different situations in which people cooperate. The teacher reported that many of the children listened with care, whereas others were disruptive or nonattentive. The teacher waited a short time until she caught one of the children listening. This is the scene that followed:

TEACHER: Mary, I saw that you were watching and listening to Susan as she shared with us. Susan, how did it feel to have Mary listen to you?
SUSAN: (smiling at Mary) It felt good when she listened to me.
TEACHER: When you listen to me, I feel good inside, too. I want to share with you, and when I look up and see your eyes, I know that you are listening to me.

The teacher continued the meeting in the same way, discussing cooperation and commenting on listening behavior. The next day she and the children had a discussion about listening. She asked them how they knew when they were being listened to. The teacher was pleased to discover that they were able to identify good listening behavior. Together, they began to construct a list of rules for class meeting time: (1) Look at people when they are speaking. (2) Sit still and be silent when someone is speaking. (3) Everyone should get a chance to share. These rules were then printed on a big sheet of paper and hung in the block corner where the class had its meeting.

Simply making rules, even with democratic participation, does not, of course, ensure that all children will follow them. In fact, the teacher reported that the very next day the class had a lot disruption, particularly by two boys, who were talking, playing with blocks, and in general disturbing others around them. What should teachers do in circumstances like this? If they discipline the unruly children (which may sometimes be necessary), they run the risk of reinforcing the view of the classroom as a place where the teacher commands and children obey, or else.

Teacher Norton handled this situation by asking the group to share the authority role: "Yesterday, the class agreed on a list of rules. Today, we have some people who are not following them. How can we, together, solve this problem?" After discussing possible solutions, the class decided to add a fourth rule to its list: A person will be asked to leave the group if, after one reminder, that person continues not to follow the rules. Significantly, the reminder could be delivered by either the teacher or another child—another sharing of authority. Children asked to leave the meeting had to go to a quiet activity elsewhere. "After a couple of days of leaving the meeting, these children joined the group successfully," reported the teacher. "Later we made an agreement that if any people were not able to follow the rules on a particular day, they would leave the circle on their own." Authority sharing thus led to the development of children's own acceptance of and compliance with rules they had helped make.

Providing Support Structures for Children

Setting rules and consequences for breaking them does more than enable children to participate in building a social order in the classroom. It also provides a support structure, an organizational feature of the social environment that helps children function at their best. Rules provide a structure, a form that shapes or "holds" individual and group behavior.

Frequently, when children do not meet the responsibilities assigned them, teachers conclude that they are "not ready," not at the stage of development where they can handle those responsibilities. This misleading half-truth is a distorted application of developmental theory. It is true that young children have a strong tendency to be egocentric. They may not be able to listen to one another in a class meeting, for example, without clear, posted rules, a system for taking turns, a short meeting time, a small group, defined personal space (a chair or a carpet square) around the circle, lots of teacher reinforcement for good listening, and so on. *With* these support structures, however, they can learn over time to listen to and interact with one another. For this reason, early childhood teachers, like any good educators, need to think of themselves as experimenters trying out different strategies to determine which enable children to operate at the cutting edge of their developmental capacity.

With this in mind, let us return to Gloria Norton and her class of kindergartners. Not fully satisfied with their behavior in circle meeting, she introduced further support structures. She proposed a Talk Ticket and a new rule, which was accepted by the children: Only the person with the Talk Ticket can speak. The Talk Ticket was handed from child to child around the circle, with a "pass" option. This new system, according to the teacher, encouraged more participation and better listening.

To sharpen listening skills further, Gloria Norton often invited a child to paraphrase what another had said. To help reticent children begin to participate, she frequently provided a sentence stem cue at the beginning of a meeting: "A time I helped someone ___," "If I found some money in our class, I would ___," "A project I would like to do in class ___." In addition to sharing meetings, the class had many planning meetings, in which the teacher and the children planned parties and project days, the results of which please everyone. Thus, even five year olds, properly guided, can take on the social responsibility of being consultants to the curriculum.

This teacher clearly gave her kindergarten children many real responsibilities of the kind that stimulate social and moral growth.

By suggesting and eliciting new rules as needs arose, she helped them understand that rules are living, evolving instruments of human purpose. And at the same time that she challenged her children to engage in democratic decision making, she did a good deal of guiding, structuring, and supporting. Democratizing the early childhood classroom does not mean less leadership or authority for the teacher but rather leadership and authority of a different kind.

Democracy with Preschoolers

Can this sort of participatory democracy be done with even younger children? Many teachers report that it can. Fern Cohen, for example, ran a nursery school for four year olds in her home. She had ten children in the morning, and ten in the afternoon. She asked each group to suggest the rules they should have for their classroom. To her surprise, the children took up this task with energy and enthusiasm. Here are the rules that the two groups came up with:

1. No punching.
2. No fighting.
3. No running (teacher's suggestion).
4. Don't stick your tongue out.
5. Don't hurt the cat.
6. You shouldn't grab things.
7. You shouldn't break things.
8. When you're finished playing with your toys, put them back on the shelf.
9. Put covers on the markers.
10. Don't throw a toy.
11. Don't steal toys.
12. Don't pull down your pants.

13. Don't put paint on the toilet paper.

14. Don't stand on the chairs.

15. Eat over your plate.

16. No spitting.

17. Don't talk mean.

We offer several observations about these rules. First, it is obvious that four year olds see their world as full of opportunities to do evil. The teacher who wonders where to find topics for class discussion can rest assured that there is plenty of grist for the moral mill. Second, the "Do not's" are far easier for four year olds to formulate than the "Do's"; they need help with the latter. Third, although some rules ("Don't steal toys" and "Don't talk mean") have a more salient moral dimension than others ("Eat over your plate" and "Put covers on the markers"), all of the suggested rules deal with behaviors that have some moral meaning. ("If you drop the food on the tables or floor, somebody has a mess to clean up." "If you leave the covers off the markers, they'll dry out and be ruined for everyone else.") To draw out and develop children's understandings of the moral meanings of these different behaviors, each rule, or cluster of similar rules, warrants a probing discussion: "Why shouldn't you grab or break things, or steal toys?" "Why shouldn't you hurt the cat or talk mean?" "Why should you put things back when you're finished with them?" "Is it ever right to punch or fight? What can you do instead that's fair?"

A fourth observation is that we can hear in these four year olds' rules the clear echoes of adult exhortations. Are these children parroting what they have been told by grown-ups time and again? In one sense, they are. But in another, more important sense, they are not. Although the content of their rules may be the old admonitions of adult authority, the process is new and exciting. Someone is asking them what *they* think the rules should be. They feel, therefore, a new sense of ownership of the rules. They experience them as *theirs*. And in the case of these children, that feeling showed up unmistakably in their social-moral behavior. The teacher reported that by the end of the week, the children were constantly reminding one another about their rules and creating new ones:

> Quite spontaneously, they would say things like, "Fern, sharing cookie cutters is a rule!" and "I know a good rule—no pinching, screaming, or yelling." They were very proud of their ability to come up with these new rules. We daily added the new ones to our list. During play, I could hear children talking about rules they had at home, for example, "When we don't treat our toys nice, Mom says to treat them nice—that's a rule!" and "My mom says, 'Don't smack your lips!' That's part of our rules." The children have become very much aware that rules exist inside and outside of the classroom. Parents even mention that their children are talking about rules at home, saying things like "You have to have rules, you know."

The Developmental Benefits of Group Decision Making

We have urged teachers to involve even young children in group decision making about the life of the classroom. As teachers who have tried it attest, this process takes time, patience, and persistence. What makes the commitment worth it? What are the benefits for the teacher and children? We submit that there are several. First, each child can come to feel a sense of participation in and responsibility for what goes on in the classroom. Such a sense of responsibility and participation has been found to be an important determinant of moral development.

Second, the teacher's moral authority in the democratic classroom is based not simply on her status as an adult (though that certainly remains one source of her authority) or on her power to discipline but, more important, on her ability to represent and promote within the classroom the legitimate interests of group members (for example, their interest in fair treatment for all). Stated another way, the teacher is, through group decision making, returning a real measure of authority to the children. To be sure, the teacher always retains a special responsibility of holding the group accountable to a standard of fairness, ensuring a reasonable conformity to the rules of the wider institutional environment, and the like. But to the extent that children are participating in formulating at least some of the rules that affect their lives, they are required to take the viewpoint of the rule maker, something that children in nondemocratic settings do not normally do.

Third, making rules a matter of collective decision sows the first seeds of moral community. Children can begin to feel a sense of belonging to a group in which each person has positive worth and has the right to speak and be heard, and where people try to be fair to one another without being forced to do so by adult authority.

Fourth, when children feel responsibility for the rules of the classroom and part of the group that makes them, they are more likely to respect the rules in their behavior than when they have no hand in making or enforcing them. Morality begins to become internal rather than external. As a third-grade girl said to her teacher, "It feels weird to break your own rules. . . . It's like disobeying your own self!"

Fifth, as children's felt responsibility, sense of membership in the community, and actual behavior change, so too does the moral atmosphere of the classroom. Moral atmosphere can be defined as the stage of the norms of behavior expectations in the group. This group stage, in turn, has real impact on the ongoing development of social-moral reasoning and behavior of individual children.

Using Conflict to Promote Social-Moral Development

Democratic decision making about classroom rules is one way to foster the social-moral development of individual children and the group's development into a just community. Group meetings, however, tend to tax the limits of young children's ability to sit still and pay attention. Experienced teachers know better than to overuse them. What other avenues are open for stimulating social-moral growth?

The spontaneous interpersonal conflicts of the classroom offer excellent opportunities to promote both social and moral reasoning and behavior application. A moment's reflection tells us that every social conflict involves role taking (social reasoning) and fairness (moral reasoning). When a conflict occurs between two children, there is almost always an issue of misunderstanding. Each child does not see the other's point of view. In discussing points of view, each child may begin to understand the thinking of the other. Beyond issues of understanding, however, social conflicts always involve the question "Who is right?" If two children are in conflict, there is an issue of fairness. Can a way be found to meet the legitimate claims of both children?

When children have a conflict, then, the teacher has three tasks: helping them understand each other's point of view; helping them work out a fair solution, one that takes into account both points of view (which will not always mean a 50–50 compromise, since one child's claim may be more legitimate than another's); helping them learn the behavior skills needed to solve their problems without the intervention of an adult. To illustrate this process in action, consider the following vignette, supplied by Julie Morrow, a prekindergarten teacher in an inner-city program for low-income children. Scott and Brian, both about four and one-half years of age, are working at the Playdoh table. Scott is cutting out heart shapes, Brian is making fishes. Scott puts down his cutter and grabs the fish cutter from Brian's hand, saying, "I want this!" Brian quickly grabs it back. Scott then grabs it again, and a tug-of-war ensues as Scott stamps his feet and whines, "I want the fish!" At this point the teacher, who has been watching the conflict develop, intervenes.

TEACHER: Okay, what's the trouble here?
BRIAN: I was using the fish, and Scott tried to grab it away!
SCOTT: I want the fish!

TEACHER: Okay, let's cool down. Scott, show me what you did when you wanted the fish. (Scott takes hold of the fish cutter and unsuccessfully tries to pull it away.) What does Brian do when you try to grab the fish cutter?

SCOTT: Holds on tighter.

TEACHER: That's right. And how does he feel when you try to grab it?

SCOTT: Mad.

TEACHER: What's a fair way of solving this problem?

BRIAN: Share.

TEACHER: Okay. (Turning to Scott) Scott, I'm going to show you what to do when you want somebody to share with you. Watch what happens when I ask Brian the *nice* way if I can use the fish cutter. (Then to Brian, making a point of keeping her hands at her sides) Brian, may I *please* use the fish cutter? (Brian then gives her the fish as Scott looks on in surprise.) (To Scott) What did I do that you didn't do?

SCOTT: You said please, and you didn't grab neither.

TEACHER: I bet if you said please and didn't grab from Brian, he would give you the fish cutter.

SCOTT: Brian, can I *please* have a turn with the fish?

To Scott's delight, Brian gives him the fish cutter. The teacher commented, "They played together cooperatively for the rest of the play time. Many other similar incidents have occurred in my class where I have used this approach with positive results."

What were the critical features of this teacher's role as conciliator and moral educator? In addition to promoting role taking and moving the children toward a fair solution, she taught Scott a social skill that he apparently did not have: the simple act of saying please. As a result, he now has at least one strategy for inviting cooperation from a peer. He has learned that words can be more powerful than force. And he is beginning to learn that he cannot impose his will on others but must instead consider their points of view and elicit their consent. These are obviously all important social and moral learnings for a child.

Note, too, that this teacher used a combination of asking and showing. She began by posing questions that got the children to think. This is a vital first step in a developmental approach. Once the cognitive wheels were turning, the teacher proceeded to her minidemonstration of how to ask for something. Asking questions first gets the child ready to assimilate the lesson offered. This ask–then show sequence both respects children's capacity as problem solvers and allows the adult to teach children important social insights and skills that they might not develop on their own. A developmental constructivist approach to social-moral education does not mean that children have to discover everything on their own. Directly instructed in a new skill or insight, they are in fact better equipped to function independently as they make their way through their social world. The teacher need not feel embarrassed about the direct act of teaching.

Scott's use of the new skill he learned had a happy outcome; he got the fish cutter. Saying please does not, of course, always yield such satisfying results. Teachers can help children become better social problem solvers by teaching them many "words to say":

Making a request: "Can I please have a short turn? I'll give it back in just a minute."

Inviting conflict resolution: "Can we make a compromise?"

Challenging behavior: "Is that fair?" (to a child who will not share or take turns)

Giving positive feedback: "Thanks for sharing!"

Giving negative feedback: "I don't like it when you grab! You should ask!"

Offering a compromise: "I'll take a short turn, then you can take a turn!"

These social competencies not only can solve the immediate social conflict but can have long-range, general benefits as well. They contribute to a positive moral atmosphere in the classroom. They foster cooperative social interactions of the kind that give children access to one another's viewpoints and ideas. This ongoing interplay of perspectives, as we have pointed out, is an essential condition for social and moral growth.

Fostering Moral Community Among Children

So far we have talked mostly about the justice side of the just community and only tangentially about the community side. Making rules and solving conflicts can certainly be seen as a form of cooperation and a step toward the creation of a moral community. But they are not enough. People can make rules and negotiate conflicts and still not come to know or like or help one another. There is not much human support or warmth in merely being fair. As one teacher commented, "The development of a bond of caring within the class is more fundamental to me than the development of a fairness ethic. There is not enough real feeling in a fairness ethic for it to be the basis of a successful community."

If not from fairness alone, whence comes a sense of community? The source of community can be found within the word itself. A feeling of *unity*, of connectedness, of being part of a larger whole, this is its root meaning. To be a member of a human community in this sense is to identify, emotionally as well as intellectually, with something larger than oneself. Teachers refer to this kind of identification when they speak of trying to develop a "class spirit" or "group feeling."

The contribution of moral development theory is to try to move a sense of community beyond the status of a nebulous concept and give it clearer moral and psychological meaning. A community becomes moral when its sense of unity springs from a shared commitment to implicit or explicit moral values. The psychological impact of that shared commitment can be enormous. Individuals no longer stand alone in their moral convictions but rather as members of a group that both supports them and holds them accountable to their common values. To think of the individual's social-moral functioning in these terms is to inform a theory of individual human development with the perspective of social psychology.

What does all of this mean for the classroom? How can a teacher of young children forge the bonds of community? One way, perhaps the most powerful, is to nurture the value of responsibility for one another's welfare. The teacher can encourage children to help one another in their individual interactions and support them when they do. But if helpfulness is to become a group value, a community norm, it must be developed and acted on within the context of the group.

A teacher can foster a group's concern for the welfare of its members in at least two ways. The first is to raise a group issue that affects everyone in the group to one degree or another. This is what happened among the third graders who formulated a group rule for solving social conflicts to "make this a better class." When a classroom is filled with strife, everyone suffers; and when it is characterized by harmony, everyone benefits. A second way to foster a sense of social responsibility is to make the group a source of help for any individual member. If some children in the class are new to the school, for example, a teacher can say, "How can we make our new members feel at home here? What can we do to make them feel part of the class?"

Even young children can respond to this kind of appeal. Nell Woomancy, a kindergarten teacher, in fact found that her children, otherwise restless, paid closest attention and contributed the most in circle meetings when she posed the question, "Who has a problem they would like other people to help them solve?" All the discussion then focused on the one child's problem until a solution was reached.

At what age can children begin to participate in this kind of caring community? The conventional wisdom, supported by at least some of the research, would say that prekindergarten is too early an age to expect children to be able to orient to the needs of others. That view is called into question, however, by the experience of teachers. Colleen Peterson, a Head Start teacher in a poor rural area, recounted a meeting with her children that suggests what young children are capable of when they are guided by a skilled teacher and acting on a real problem that matters to them.

The problem in this case was a four-year-old boy named Billy, soon to go into the hospital for an operation. "As the day approached," the teacher recounted, "Billy became noticeably more sullen and preoccupied. He seemed to avoid his best friends and to shy away from even his favorite group projects." In a conversation with the teacher, Billy revealed that he was afraid the operation would "hurt," but he would say no more. The teacher decided to talk about Billy's surgery in class meeting: "I thought that most of the children were feeling hurt by Billy's deliberate avoidance of all of us and also that Billy was not happy with his relationship with the children."

Billy's feelings and behavior were obviously a sensitive subject for whole-group discussion, requiring the most sensitive handling by the teacher. In the meeting excerpt that follows, note her artful and multifaceted role: drawing out Billy, drawing out other children's feelings about his avoidance behavior, getting them to think about why he might be acting that way, carefully reflecting what children say, relating Billy's experience to that of other children, and guiding the discussion gently to its positive conclusion.

TEACHER: Someone has told me that he doesn't like the room the way it is right now. He has told me it is not a happy place to be. Does anyone else feel this way?

BLAKE: Yeah, I do. Billy don't talk to me. He don't let me sit by him at snack.

TEACHER: You feel bad that Billy doesn't want you to sit by him at snack?

BLAKE: Yeah.

TEACHER: Billy, is there a reason you won't let Blake sit by you at snack?

BILLY: I don't want him to. I don't want to sit by anyone.

TEACHER: I think that Billy is feeling bad. Does anyone know why Billy is feeling this way?

MICHELLE: He doesn't like us.

TEACHER: Is that true, Billy, that you don't like anyone here?

BILLY: No.

SUSAN: Well, he doesn't play with us, and that's not nice.

ERIC: I think he's sad because he got to go in the hospital.

TEACHER: Billy, are you sad because you are going to go to the hospital?

BILLY: It will hurt. Eric told me it does. And I want to go to school.

TEACHER: You're afraid you will miss a lot of school if you go to the hospital?

BILLY: Yes (long silence). And you will forget me.

TEACHER: You think that we'll forget about you when you're in the hospital, away from school?

BILLY: Yes.

TEACHER: I don't think that will happen.

ERIC: That won't happen because I will miss you.

TEACHER: Will anyone else miss Billy when he's in the hospital?

BLAKE: Yeah, I will.

SUSAN: If he starts bein' nice again, I'll miss him.

MICHELLE: When I was in the hospital, everyone missed me a lot.

TEACHER: I think Michelle knows what it is like to be in the hospital. You have been in the hospital many times, haven't you, Michelle?

MICHELLE: Yes, I have.

TEACHER: Michelle, when you were in the hospital, did many people visit you or send you cards?

MICHELLE: Just my Mommy and Daddy.

TEACHER: Would you have liked it if all of us had known you then and had done something nice, like send you cards, when you were in the hospital?

MICHELLE: (Emphatically) YES!

TEACHER: Do you think maybe we could do something like that for Billy when he is in the hospital?

ERIC: Yes, we better do that, 'cause he's our friend, and we should be nice to him and try to make him feel better (followed by unanimous agreement and a smile from Billy).

The children did indeed all make Billy Get Well and Miss You cards when he was in the hospital. The teacher remarked, "I had very positive feelings about this class meeting and its outcome. I had never known the extent to which my children were able to sympathize with and feel compassion for others. Too often I attributed to the classic egocentrism of three and four year olds what was, in reality, just an absence of situations in which they might demonstrate their feelings."

We view this teacher's experience as further attesting the importance of providing environmental support structures, like a well-guided class meeting. Such structures enable children to use their available developmental capacities to the fullest and to engage in the kinds of interactions that will promote their further social and moral development.

Cooperation and Conflict

In any group, some interpersonal tensions or conflicts almost always occur at some point when social interaction, however cooperative, is intensified. More interactions mean more things to disagree about. These "bumps," however, are part of a healthy social-moral curriculum. Having a cooperative classroom does not mean trying to eliminate conflict, just as it does not mean eliminating individual and competitive learning modes, which both have motivational value and a place in the educational process. Resolving conflict requires role taking and moral judgment. The experience of conflict is therefore an important spur for social and moral development. The goal of cooperative learning is to help create a context, a community ethos, in which conflict is engaged and resolved in a spirit of fairness and mutual concern.

In the following example of conflict, from the University of Houston Human Development Laboratory School, the teacher attempts to mediate conflict through appeal to fairness and democratic agreement. The teacher is playing the game Concentration with two five-year-old boys. The children's self-interests clash, and they struggle to resolve the problem of turns and other issues. The thought of the two boys, Yousef and Christopher, ranges from Stage 0 to Stage 2. The teacher invites the boys to find the matching pairs of animals and reads the rules from the lid of the box:

TEACHER: Boys, who should go first?
YOUSEF: Me.
CHRISTOPHER: Me.
TEACHER: You both want to go first.
YOUSEF: "Bubble gum, bubble gum" (begins rhyme, pointing to each player in turn).
CHRISTOPHER: I don't like to do "bubble gum, bubble gum."
YOUSEF: Let's take a vote.
CHRISTOPHER: No, there aren't enough people who want to vote.

The moral atmosphere of the classroom is reflected in Yousef's response to this conflict situation. Teachers in the Human Development Laboratory School had worked hard to give children methods of settling disputes through the use of impartial procedures such as voting and rhymes (such as "eeney, meeney, miney, moe") that designate players successively and in which the last player designated wins. Christopher, too, focuses on the method for deciding rather than on what he wants.

> TEACHER: Okay, so far we've talked about "bubble gum, bubble gum" or voting, and you don't like either of those. What do you think, Chris- Christopher?
> CHRISTOPHER: I think that I'll just pick who goes first.
> YOUSEF: No.
> CHRISTOPHER: I'll just pick.
> YOUSEF: No, I said that first. And then you came and speaked when I was speaking. So, I'm just gonna do "bubble gum, bubble gum."
> CHRISTOPHER: Okay, but that sure does disturb me.

Christopher's insistence on what he wants brings another impasse, with each child repeating his solution. Christopher grudgingly agrees to go along with Yousef but expresses his unhappiness. The problem for the teacher, then, is to respect Christopher's feelings but try to get him to consider a (more mature) view of fairness.

> TEACHER: Do you think "bubble gum, bubble gum" would be all right with you, Christopher?
> CHRISTOPHER: It's not all right with me, but if he wants to do it (shrugs).
> TEACHER: Do you think your picking would be fair, Christopher?
> YOUSEF: No, I don't think Christopher should pick.

With the impasse reasserted, the teacher continues to give the responsibility to the children for coming to agreement, but she upholds the value of mutual agreement. By respecting the ideas of both children, she expresses the idea that conflict resolution should consider everyone's feelings.

TEACHER: Let's see if y'all can decide on something that you both like.

CHRISTOPHER: I just wanta pick somebody. I don't like that "bubble gum, bubble gum."

YOUSEF: All right. Who says to do "bubble gum, bubble gum"? (He raises his hand.)

CHRISTOPHER: Nobody, I don't.

YOUSEF: (Turns to teacher) Do you wish to do "bubble gum"?

TEACHER: Well, if I vote, then whatever I say will happen because you both disagree.

CHRISTOPHER: It's okay with me if you do whatever you want because you're the adult.

Christopher's response is to identify fairness with whatever the adult authority wants. But the teacher upholds the idea of the importance of agreement among players.

TEACHER: But y'all are playing the game, too. I think y'all should decide, too. Do you have any other ideas, Yousef?

CHRISTOPHER: Well, I'd just like to pick.

YOUSEF: Well, you need to vote, too. So?

CHRISTOPHER: Well, Yousef, the only thing that doesn't disturb me is "eeney, meeney, miney, moe." You can say that, but not "bubble gum, bubble gum."

YOUSEF: Okay. "Eeney, meeney, miney, moe, catch a tiger by the toe. If he hollers, let him go. Eeney, meeney, miney (stops as he realizes that "moe" will land on Christopher). Wait a second.

CHRISTOPHER: No, no. You can't just stop.

YOUSEF: Wait. Let me pick somebody now.

Yousef's acceptance of a procedure agreeable to Christopher as well as himself turns out to be rooted in the expectation that a rhyme procedure will get him what he wants! When he miscalculates, it is Christopher's turn to defend the rhyme procedure when it suits *his* self-interest! The teacher tries to uphold the agreement made between the two boys on using a rhyme procedure to resolve the conflict:

> TEACHER: How did that work out? What happened with "eeney, meeney, miney, moe"?
> YOUSEF: He was gonna get first.
> CHRISTOPHER: Wait, now let me do it (repeats the rhyme and "moe" lands on the teacher). You can go first.
> TEACHER: That's what you want me to do?
> CHRISTOPHER: Yeah.
> YOUSEF: Yeah.

Letting the teacher go first is an acceptable solution to both boys, so the teacher goes first. Even though the eventual agreement is based on deference to the teacher's authority, it is a solution arrived at through a process of exchange of viewpoints and autonomous decision making of the two children.

Opportunities for Cooperative Learning

Opportunities for cooperative learning are everywhere in the classroom. One teacher, for example, incorporated cooperation into formal lessons, doing group terrariums for their study of plants and a class mural for their study of the circus. Teachers of young children have engaged them in cooperative block building, cooperative drawing, cooperative puzzles, and various other forms of cooperative problem solving. Teachers of elementary-age children have found many ways to foster cooperation and teach academic skills at the same time: partner learning (the smallest social unit and a good way to begin), small group projects in subjects such as science and social studies, team research, and even team testing. Teachers of all levels have successfully involved their pupils in cooperative activities such as class plays, class newspapers, and class projects to help the wider school or community.

To reiterate, the moral curriculum and the academic curriculum can be two sides of the same coin. When students work together in a cooperative mode, their enthusiasm for learning and academic performance significantly increases.

Summary

We have argued in this chapter that there is much that teachers can do, even in the early childhood years, to make the spirit of participatory democracy part of the "bone and blood" of children's lives in the classroom. By building a just community, teachers are engaged in the most important task of education: helping children develop the intellectual, social, and moral competence, the habits of thought and action, on which the survival of social democracy and individual human welfare so vitally depend.

. . . .

8

Curriculum and Behavior Problems
Giving Children a Voice

Susan Steinsieck and Kim E. Myers

*Both Chapter 7 and this one remind me of my experi-
ence observing a master teacher, Judy Lazrus, and
her first-grade classroom, where community building
through giving each child a voice was the curriculum.
I saw this in action during a morning meeting when
children listened intently to one another telling about
their bedtime routines. The discussion was filled with
sharing of the troublesome fantasies that make going
to bed so difficult for young children, fantasies of
witches, monsters, snakes, and the like. But it was
also filled with active empathizing and helpful suggestions for dealing with the fantasies (placing a flashlight
under a pillow, concentrating on particular thoughts,
and so on). The sharing was remarkable but hardly
an accident, for in this classroom the children were
used to being encouraged and rewarded for listening
and sharing. Here is how Judy Lazrus has described
the encouraging process:*

The purpose of our discussions, which we have
during morning meeting on Thursday, is to take a
universal or group interest, concern, or concept
and see how we each view the topic. Each child's

view is influenced by his or her experience, temperament, family, culture, etc. Children see that some have similar feelings and some do not. And they hear an array of strategies for coping with the issues that children and adults cope with—everything from what your family does when there is a bug in your house to coping with feelings of loss, fear, or rejection. We try to look at all angles. Not just have you ever been teased but when have you teased, whom do you tease, why? (The consensus on that one is "it's fun."). Discussion topics come from the theme, kids, and parents. Sometimes it has to do with classroom observation. Seeing cliques develop might inspire a discussion on "Have you ever felt left out?"

Getting children to talk and listen begins day one. Noticing when children are being kind to each other. Offering opportunities to respond to others, being explicit about our expectations. We sit in a circle so we can see each other. We sit up to show respect. We look at the person who is talking so he or she will feel listened to. We respond to the topic seriously so people won't be embarrassed to express their feelings. We try not to do things that will take the spotlight off of the person whose turn it is because everyone needs to get their share of the group's recognition and attention. The group provides support and recognition to its members.

Each morning meeting has a group function. Monday, Wednesday, and Friday are news days. Kids share news or things from their lives. When everyone is done sharing, the group comments around. "This is for Ryan, I like your dog.

Where did you get it?" "This is for Tessa, I'm sorry
your fish died." The person on the receiving end
of the comment acknowledges it with thanks, or
whatever is appropriate.

*In teacher Lazrus's class, then, children learn to care
for one another by the way they listen and share.
And, in so doing, each comes to develop a sense of
being an important member of a community, a sense
that helps children modify their behavior problems in
order to do a better job of fitting in.*

   *In Steinsieck and Myers's thoughtful discus-
sion of how we can develop curricula so as to give
children a voice, which, in turn, supports their
becoming members of the classroom community, we
see the developmental approach: the teachers share
control and become partners with children in creating
curricula. And here we see materials used within this
partnership to capture and organize children's interests
to the point where the children gain self-control.*

                                     W. George Scarlett

In a kingdom, one voice rules, not because it is right but because
the king has power. Likewise, in a classroom there can be a single, dominant voice, the teacher's voice, because the teacher too
has power. But if students are given a voice and if their voices com-
bine to form a chorus, there will be richer learning and greater harmony. In this chapter, we try to show how our approach to
curriculum can work to give children both an individual and a collective voice and, in so doing, create a climate that expands a child's
ability to communicate, encourages constructive behaviors, and
works against behavior problems.

   At the heart of our approach to curriculum is a partnership
between teacher and child, a partnership that builds on the children's
interests and guides them to use materials to find their voices and

collaborate with others. Materials and interests are starting points. If teachers listen, they can best discover what matters to the children and how to support their development.

In our kindergarten classroom, we supply children with a rich array of materials from which to choose. Our drawing table is a wooden door attached to four-inch legs. On nearby shelves, we stock craypas, pencils, crayons, markers, chalk, scotch tape, colored masking tapes, staplers, hole punches, fasteners, and scissors. We make available eighty-pound drawing paper in at least two sizes, 9"× 12" and 12"× 18." For dramatic play, we have constructed a small cave, a loft, and a puppet theater with red velvet curtains; we also supply a host of props for creating stories: skirts and capes, plates and food, and plastic animals and puppets. Small and big blocks are close at hand. The painting easel is always available during project time, as are sand and water tables. There is a big table for collage (the shelves are stocked with a variety of papers, recycled materials, and wood) and clay work.

The use of the curriculum to help children with behavior problems is illustrated in the stories we tell here. First, however, we focus on our use of one activity and material, namely, model building with clay. Our goal is to clarify just how providing materials to children with behavior problems can give them a voice that allows them to connect with others.

Clay

Clay is a wonderfully versatile material. Children's use of clay gives tangible results, instant feedback, and satisfaction. Their first experience with clay includes the tactile pleasures of pounding, squeezing, pushing, and stretching. They spread the clay around the work space in messy, pleasurable ways. They notice that clay sticks under their fingernails and to their hands; they notice it dries to a powder and fills the grooves of their work boards. "Ooooh, this clay is cold to touch." "Feel how smooth I made the cake, like ice." "If you were working as hard as I am, your hands would be this dirty too!" "Hey, look at my thumb print. I put my thumb there, and it made a little hole." Whether generally responsive to tactile experiences or not, children enjoy squeezing the cool clay through their fingers. They quickly transform clay balls into towers, mountains, bricks, or snakes.

We use low-fire white and terra cotta clay. Children work the clay on small wooden boards (12"× 12") cut from a plywood sheet. They use toothpicks for drawing in clay and popsicle sticks for smoothing and attaching. They make their own slip (clay and water mixed yields glue for clay). Children also glaze their work using low-fire underglazes. Teachers apply the "shiny" glaze. This diverse set of materials offers children opportunities to express themselves in many ways, including through mark making, storytelling, playacting, and model building.

In the didactic process we follow, every piece produced by the children needs to be valued as evidence that learning has occurred. No false praise is needed; children sense hypocrisy with amazing acuity. Some children actively seek validation of each construction they devise; others work quietly and then leave without showing any need for affirmation. The teacher must be sensitive to individual differences and respond appropriately. Sometimes this valuing reaps tangible results, as the following example illustrates:

James spent twenty minutes flattening a piece of clay, which he then cut into dozens of tiny little squares. After finishing, he left without a word. A week later, James wandered over to the windowsill where we keep recently fired work. "Wow, you cooked all these pieces. You know, I was hoping you would because I need them." We could have easily tossed these little pieces, especially since they were crude compared to what James usually produced. Fortunately, we did value, save, and fire them, thus giving James a chance to tell us what they meant to him. We discovered they were his "treasures" for an elaborate "bird-camping game." "Gee, these treasures are just perfect," he said with enormous pride.

We keep talking with the children as they work; they tell us and their classmates what they are doing and for what purpose. Through this talking and listening, their final products take on both personal and collective meaning.

Perhaps the strongest evidence of the power of the curriculum to stimulate collective meaning comes from the conversations among the children as they work. These are vigorous, highly positive social interactions. While the children work, themes emerge that interest everyone (for example, coins, treasures, families, animals, and space creatures), and these themes take on lives of their own. "Now look. You see how I made this here. It's a hole." "How'd you do that?" "What's it for?" "It's a snake." "No, I think it's a ___." So goes the discussion until the children return to their own clay to work on their own holes: one for a trap, another for treasure, and another for a "worm's home."

These examples clarify our main point: The curriculum has to do with engaging children in the productive use of materials and stimulating conversation that creates collective, as well as personal, meanings. When the curriculum succeeds, children engage in valuable learning experiences. A climate is created that works against behavior problems.

Curriculum and Children with Behavior Problems

Having introduced how we help children work with clay, we turn to our first example of how this work relates to behavior problems.

> Gregory stood rigid, his fists clenched, jaw locked, breath forced and deliberate, all signals conveying his anger. He had just kicked over a block structure, injuring a classmate in the process. His eyes shone with satisfaction, "See, I destroyed it. And if you don't be nice to me, I'll do it again." He stood as if in a trance, squinting and breathing heavily. His body shivered with intensity. No matter what we did or said, we could not calm him, so we sent him to calm himself in a separate part of the room.

This oft-repeated behavior came to characterize Gregory's relationships with us and with his peers. We found ourselves caught in an unsatisfactory pattern: Gregory would act out, then he would be sent to the bench where he would sit until returning to play and to acting out again, thus beginning a new cycle.

Instead of continuing this pattern, we tried to break it by focusing on Gregory's interests and on finding ways to engage Gregory in our developmental curriculum. Through watching and interacting with Gregory, we discovered his interest in coins. Most days he would bring in several coins. At first, we seldom noticed them except when he used them as part of a trap or weapon. Once we began noticing and once we took an interest, Gregory started talking with us more freely. Soon, during project time, he would line up his coins to show them to us and answer our questions.

Having spotted Gregory's interest, we showed him books that contained dazzling photos and sketches of coins, and we encouraged him to bring in more coins. He responded with enthusiasm, and soon he shared his vast collection at group time. To our delight, his classmates were interested, especially in the coins' markings and designs.

In this opening process, we encouraged Gregory to express his interest in coins by making coins out of clay. He responded by making hundreds of coins. Often he became so absorbed that he worked for twenty to thirty minutes in one sitting. With the patience of a watchmaker, he carefully flattened small balls of clay, tapped the edges to form perfect discs, then etched their surfaces with apt and intriguing patterns. As the year progressed, Gregory's coins became intricate and detailed. Through patient tinkering, he mastered the material and refined each step in the production process. Gregory got strong personal gratification from his work. We lauded his creations. Happily, so did his peers.

Gregory had been accustomed to working alone, but his modeling in clay brought him into contact with others, and that contact, in turn, led to positive interactions and beginning friendships. We are convinced all of this would not have happened were it not for his work with clay. Before clay, Gregory could not express himself with words. Before clay, he had no voice. His disruptive behavior, his striking out, and his moving around at the periphery of the classroom all indicated that he had no voice. But the coin making gave him a voice and a way to enter the community.

As teachers, we did our part by responding to his work, by handling his creations with care, and by putting them on display. Most important, we sustained a dialogue that kept him engaged:

> TEACHER: I see you have made five little coins and two big coins. How are you making them bigger? Can you show me?
> GREGORY: You see, you need to take a little more clay to make these. These big ones are the real treasure.
> TEACHER: Wow, these coins are from a treasure! Tell me about the treasure.
> GREGORY: You see, these coins (pointing to the small coins) are the ones leading to the treasure. You think you found the treasure, but you didn't really. If you go on through the path and don't get burned by the fire pit, you could find the real treasure, the BIG ones!"

Stimulated by these dialogues, Gregory created fanciful stories of dangerous adventures and treasure maps. By that time, coins and treasure maps had become an expanding theme that held a strong attraction for the other children as well. In one planned activity, using large pieces of paper charred around the edges to resemble an old map, pairs of students created guiding marks for the location of treasure. To our delight, the collaboration continued beyond this activity, and the relationships blossomed throughout the year.

But clay provided Gregory with more than a way to connect with others. It provided him also with a way to lead. We were rewarded by witnessing at the clay table his first tentative steps at leading.

One afternoon, Gregory called to several boys, "Hey guys, do you want to make ninja stars. They're really cool." Five boys charged the clay table and crowded around Gregory. "Look, I'll show you how. Get some clay. Everyone got some? Okay, first you take a piece like this, and then you roll it like a snake. Make it thin, but not too much. You don't want it to break. Then take another piece and do the same thing. (Looking around) No, not like that. Ooops, yours broke. Here, try some more. Now put a dot of slip on this and put the other piece like that. (Peering over Nick's work and craning his neck to see) Yeah, Nick, you did it. You need to put some more like this." And so continued his lesson.

Gregory's growth did not end when he left in June. He attended the school's summer camp program, and from a fresh vantage point, we witnessed the flowering of his skills. He successfully negotiated new social interactions and developed friendships with a variety of children. He explored his environments safely and watched out for the well-being of younger children. He easily and proudly taught those who had not yet worked with clay. His interest was now directed toward the clay-modeling process itself and its creative use by others.

Through involvement in the curriculum with clay, Gregory gained self-definition, confidence, and the respect of others. In one year, he had evolved from disrupter to craftsman and, finally, to teacher. In the summer, the journey continued as Gregory left the clay table to play with his new friends on the playground.

Gregory's case is an example of our general approach to curricula and to using the curriculum to manage behavior problems. The next example illustrates how building on a child's interest and creating a curriculum out of that interest can be effective in managing behavior problems, even strange problems with clinical labels. In addition, this example illustrates how a developmental approach differs from traditional clinical approaches, which emphasize diagnoses, treatments, and labels.

Susan spun into the room and began zipping from the cubbies to the writing area to the scrounge area, all the while feverishly collecting materials and stuffing bits of foam, rubber bands, markers, and pipe cleaners into her pockets, her bag, and even her socks. Her whirling dervish entrance made each of us dizzy. Children shouted, "Susan took all the markers!" "Susan took the tape!" "Look at all the stickers Susan has!" When approached by a teacher, Susan responded, "Mine." When asked to put materials back, she implored, "But I need them." In fact, she did. Most of Susan's days were spent in this cyclone of activity focusing on collecting stuff. When Susan was on the move, other children veered away. She paid them no mind, and they left her alone.

Susan entered our classroom already marked with the diagnostic label attention deficit-hyperactivity disorder. But rather than seeing her problems through the lens of this label, we chose to see through Susan's eyes. We chose to learn about her interests, her ideas, and what she valued. We chose to respect her work.

Recognizing that Susan's collections were what she valued and what she considered her work, we set out to help her develop her collecting. One teacher asked, "What did you collect in your bag today?" "I wonder what you could do with all of this?" As a class, we read books about inventions and designed class projects. In order to give definition and structure to the activities, we provided each child with a small produce basket, each containing identical recyclable materials. On the tables for common use were different materials for attaching and joining the recyclable stuff, such as scissors, tapes, pipe cleaners, and wires. We asked children to think about attachments and movements such as folding and bending. Most important, toward our goal of structuring experiences, we set clear boundaries of personal materials and shared tools. Susan began constructing inventions out of her stuff. We asked, "Can you use this tape to put together your stuff?" Our goal was twofold: to provide Susan with plenty of stuff to gather and to help her organize her collections.

As she gathered, Susan created her own field of expertise, her own understanding of how to use materials such as paints, markers, scrounge items, and sticks and stones. Dialogue with Susan about her gathering revealed that she grasped certain mathematical concepts such as massing, sorting, and size progression as well as non-mathematical concepts such as color. Building on these concepts and her interests, we challenged Susan with sorting activities and helped her explore colors and their combinations.

We helped Susan channel her interests in socially acceptable ways. The class came to regard Susan as the guru of materials and turned to her for assistance. They knew that she knew where to find materials, and she usually complied by producing whatever other children might need. Of course, our work with Susan was painstakingly slow. Her status as a guru was not achieved overnight.

Just as Susan's gathering began to have a positive effect on her classmates, so too did her classmates begin to have a positive effect on her. At the beginning of the year, Susan would stop briefly at the clay table, scoop up materials such as a pound of clay, then bounce off to another part of the room. As the year progressed, however, Susan spent more time with clay, often watching others work.

In particular, she watched Gregory's coin making. Soon she began producing rugged ball forms, which she called her "coins." In less than a minute, she could produce a dozen such coins, which she then glazed in various colors. Each morning she went straight to the clay shelves to ask, "Do I have anything to glaze?" She would assemble an array of dishes, each containing a separate color of glaze, and spend ten, fifteen, even twenty minutes glazing.

Susan's expertise with color was soon recognized by her classmates, who subsequently spent more time glazing their own pieces or, in some cases, even asking Susan to glaze them. Finally, after firing her coins a second time, Susan would carefully wrap each coin (her "treasures," as she called them) in colorful tissue paper and present them as gifts to teachers, family members, classmates, and visitors.

Susan also created snakes and snake houses, work obviously influenced by other children's work on cobra snakes and animal houses. During the summer, she began constructing tadpole people, which caught the interest of other children, who then also began modeling clay people. Through clay, Susan began to connect with others both by following their leads and having them, in turn, follow hers.

Curriculum and Community

By late March, each of the children seemed to be flourishing in rich and exciting ways. But the class as a whole did not cohere. There was, as yet, no clear sense of community. Yes, there were pockets of children working together, and, yes, there were days that went by with a soothing tick and hum. But these smooth times were frequently interrupted by rocky times, and so we were dissatisfied. By focusing on developing each child's voice, we had placed insufficient attention on fostering a collective voice. And so we refocused our attention, once again with the help of clay.

One Thursday in March, we began a large-scale project requiring collaborative involvement from the entire class. We invited a local artist skilled in sculpture and ceramics to join us. We hoped that he would stimulate a new, qualitatively higher level of work. With this artist's guidance, we all began chucking hunks of clay onto the table: thwapping them down in gradually spreading slabs, a technique that the children had never before seen. There was a flurry of excited comments, gasps, and peals of laughter. "What are you doing?" "Whoa, did you see that piece slam into the other?" "Holy molely!" "Why are you throwing clay?" "Hey, can I try that?" The children delighted in the kinesthetic of this process, and, quickly, their creative action displaced awe and shock. "What are we going to make?" they asked. "Let's make a clay world," the artist responded. "If this is the land, what would be in it?"

The collective planning and building began. The children talked of houses, trees, animals, pathways, trains, and boats. They created as they talked, and they all talked. Children who had earlier found no occasion to choose some of the others' company now stood within inches of one another, deep in a cooperative effort. At times, we could have heard a pin drop, so hushed were the moments of creative concentration.

Everyone present was caught by the purpose and meaning of this project, and everyone invested energy, ideas, and labor toward its completion. Everyone's hands became imprinted on this island world of clay. Everyone worked under one constraint: to respect the work that existed.

With direction from the artist, the children learned new skills and techniques. They were led to higher levels of craftsmanship. They were challenged, frustrated, excited, and disappointed, and through this common, emotion-laden experience, they came to understand that the island was bigger than any one individual and better because all had contributed. Over the four days of the project's creation, comments shifted from "This is my Tyrannosaurus Rex" and "I'm making the train," to "I think I'll make a boat so that Daren's snakes can get from the big island to the smaller one" and "Can you believe this island! It's gigantic. Where are we going to put anything else?" They built connection to the island and, through it, to one another.

Along the way, we learned to communicate better with one another and we gained awareness of one another's work—so much so, for example, that David became excited about Andrew's fire dogs, two "blobs" squashed under a tree. As the children showed the island to visitors, they pointed to each child's work: "See over there is the tunnel for the train, Brian made that." "If you look really closely, you can see Jackie's little tiny dinosaur eggs." "Jason, Jack, and Catherine made that lookout tower for the man."

After the island was finished, or, rather, after it was filled up, teachers sliced it into small sections labeled with letters to create a jigsaw puzzle. The pieces were fired, glazed by the children, and fired again. Like magnets, children crowded around the display table.

Some began weaving stories of adventure about the island. Others just looked. Over the next couple of weeks, the island became an active curriculum material. Children wrote stories, drew pictures, and playacted adventures. After placing it on the floor in the dramatic play area, parents and children worked to fit the pieces together, and small groups of children played at hopping over the island. The island had provided many ways for the children to connect.

Concluding Remarks

This chapter tells the story of our developmental curriculum and its help with behavior problems. We focused on the way in which we use clay as but one example among many. We could have given equally developed examples where we used different materials and activities. The point of our discussion is not about clay but about materials and constructive curriculum activities that can help children with behavior problems. These are activities that cultivate the individual voices of children and support their hearing of one another's voices together so that their solos become a chorus.

. . . .

9

Programming, the Physical Environment, and Behavior Problems

W. George Scarlett with Kim E. Myers

This chapter completes the section on developing classrooms as a way of managing and preventing behavior problems while still supporting children's development. In this chapter, we focus on the part played by programming and the physical environment in preventing behavior problems. By programming, we mean the decisions that all teachers make in order to get themselves and a group of children from the start to the finish of the day: decisions about what kinds of activities to make available to the children and in what sequence, what kinds of rituals to employ to help make transitions go smoothly, how long group meetings should run, and so forth. Here, we are interested in defining how decisions about programming can be made with an eye toward preventing behavior problems.

This narrowing of the topic to programming as a means of preventing behavior problems leads to our focus on how programming can support young children's ability to handle the "thousand natural shocks" to which they are subjected at school: shocks from being interrupted in play, shocks from having construction materials go bad, shocks from having to sit and wait too long, and so forth. These and other felt shocks can be immediate sources of behavior problems, so preventing them through programming is our goal.

The other subject of this chapter is the physical environment, specifically, the built environment: activity corners, pathways connecting activity corners, cubbies, meeting areas, and so forth.

Here, too, our concern is with defining the role of the built environment in preventing behavior problems. When thoughtfully planned, built environments can prevent behavior problems by promoting constructive initiative, play, and work. When not thoughtfully planned, built environments can promote just the opposite.

In looking at programming and the physical environment, we examine once again rules and materials. Rules and materials were subjects in previous chapters. However, the foci in previous chapters were rules to establish justice and materials used in a curriculum. In contrast, the focus here is on procedural rules to move and organize children and on how materials are prepared, maintained, and stored.

Programming

The central idea behind seeing programming as an important way to prevent behavior problems is the provision of what Redl and Wineman (1965) so effectively described as "ego support" to prevent and manage behavior problems. This notion of ego has nothing to do with an inflated sense of self, as in "He has a big ego." Rather, it has to do with young children's ability to manage difficult feelings such as occur when they are frustrated or tempted to act impulsively. It also has to do with young children's ability to take in, evaluate, and understand reality. Providing ego support, then, has to do with providing young children the help they need to manage their feelings and understand reality. When they do not receive such help, they often misbehave.

The help provided by programming to support young egos can come in many forms. Here, we focus on just a few of the main aids, namely, rituals for helping children connect to the classroom and begin the school day, a clear and regular daily schedule, rituals for making transitions between activities and events, activities that are well organized and planned, and activities that are matched to children's abilities.

Rituals for Beginning the Day

Chapter 3, which focuses on finding security in the classroom, makes clear that there is no more important issue than helping young children feel secure and connected. That chapter also makes clear that an important aspect of helping young children feel secure is helping them separate from parents and connect to the classroom at the beginning of the day. Most early childhood teachers understand this. But not every teacher builds rituals into the daily program to help make this happen.

The most obvious ritual is that of greeting a child, every child, and making him or her feel incredibly welcome. Good teachers do this with enthusiasm and style; they also do this without interrupting the good-bye rituals between parent and child. They understand that for children to connect to the classroom, they must successfully disconnect from parents and what is outside the classroom.

Some teachers help with this disconnecting by showing children how to take control. For example, in one classroom, children were encouraged to take a position at the top of the inside climbing structure, where they could look out through a window on top of the cubbies and wave at their parents who were walking away (while waving back, of course). When the separation becomes too great and children simply cannot take control, well-run classrooms insert the ritual of a teacher holding and soothing children while helping them wave and say good-bye.

Of course, with certain early childhood programs, it is a bus and not a parent that drops children off at the beginning of the day. But there are rituals here to help children connect and feel secure. In particular, there are rituals for children to find their way from bus to cubby and from cubby to participation in the classroom.

Help with connecting to the classroom at the beginning of the day is help with managing difficult feelings around separation, but it is also help with orienting in time. Orienting in time has to do with that other meaning of ego, namely, taking in, evaluating, and understanding reality. The reality here is the reality that time is divided and organized. The day is not one big block of time. Young children know this, but their knowledge is sketchy, hence they can become disoriented and anxious or act in ways not suited to particular times. They need help marking the boundaries and making transitions. Greeting rituals and rituals to help say good-bye provide that help.

Daily Schedule

A similar situation holds for the classroom's daily schedule. There is no question that a classroom's daily schedule needs to be clear and regular in order to help children orient themselves within the time they are at school. And there is no question that this orientation helps prevent behavior problems. In well-run classrooms, children know where they are in the course of a schedule, and knowing where they are helps them know what they should be doing.

The following is an example of a classroom where the schedule was never clear and where, as a result, children were often confused and disoriented.

The general class schedule was not very clear; children did not seem to be aware of it. At the end of breakfast, children were told, "Okay, go play," but no mention was made of what specific activities were open or if, in fact, there were activities open. It seemed as though teachers had opened some activities and that others would be opened if children showed an interest. For example, one child put on a smock but then found that none of the art materials had been set up. The assistant teacher noticed and said to the head teacher, "I'm going to open sponge painting because I think they want to paint." As soon as she started to set up the sponges, paints, and paper, many more children came to the painting area than could be accommodated, causing a good deal of confusion, frustration, and anger among them.

In this classroom, poor programming in the form of a disorganized schedule promoted in children a low-level and chronic confusion, which made it hard for them to become engrossed in productive play. Here is another example of poor programming and its consequences:

> Around the middle of the morning, the classroom seemed to be in transition as teachers and assistants started to clean up, but there was no announcement of a transition, so many of the children were simply wandering around. The head teacher announced that two of the activity areas were closed. She then looked at three children and told them to find something to do. Gradually, it became clear that this really was not a transition at all but rather a time when some activities were closed as others were opening. This made for confusion. For example, one girl went to the easel, which prompted the head teacher to say, "We're not coloring today." When the girl said, "Please," the head teacher gave in and handed the girl paper and crayons. When other children came over to ask to join the girl, the head teacher handed them paper and crayons, which prompted one to say, "I thought there was no coloring." The head teacher responded with, "I know, but they made me."

Problems with scheduling can also occur when there are outside specialists working with children with special needs. Here, there are bound to be problems. No class can run exactly on schedule, so outside specialists need to show both patience and ingenuity in finding ways to fit in and integrate their own schedules into the daily schedule of the classroom. Few do this perfectly, but a good specialist can create a reasonable fit. In the following example, the fit was hardly reasonable, creating problems not only for the children with special needs but for everyone else in the classroom as well:

> A physical therapist visited the class often to work with two children in particular, but within an inclusion model (that is, other children were

encouraged to join in). As was often the case, this day she arrived without being prepared and without preparing the head teacher. While the children and head teacher were in group meeting, she interrupted several times to ask for supplies and directions as to where to carry out her special activity. Her activity took a long time to set up, and so the children had to wait much longer than usual. Naturally, they fidgeted, which elicited a good deal of reprimanding by the head teacher.

Transitions

To make any daily schedule easy for children to follow, there also have to be transition rituals. That young children need rituals to help them make transitions is well known. But knowing that young children need help is one thing and providing it is another. Here is an example of a classroom that did not give one little boy the help he needed to make a transition from play:

> Joe and Don were making a road of blocks. Joe called to a teacher, "Look how long our road is!" The assistant teacher, Diane, replied, "Wow, that's the longest road I've ever seen! Can I play in blocks with you?" "Yes, but you have to park your car here," answered Don. Just as Diane joined them, the head teacher rang the clean-up bell. Diane and Joe began to put away blocks, but Don refused, saying, "No! I don't want to clean up." He then started to kick and throw blocks. Diane responded, "Don, you need to help Joe clean up so we can have circle before we go on our field trip." Don smiled and then ran across the room laughing. Diane called after him, "Don, you have a choice, you can either help Joe clean up or you can stay at school while we are on our trip and clean up then." When Don continued to throw things, Diane grabbed him, whereupon he punched her.

In this example, Don could have used a warning that clean-up was soon to come. And perhaps, too, he could have used a stronger ritual such as his becoming the bell ringer to announce clean-up.

One of the interesting differences between classrooms with and those without well-planned programming is the way teachers express themselves in their transition rituals. In classrooms with well-planned programming, some teachers play music or sing. Others play games such as "freeze." Whatever the ritual, these teachers have a knack for making transitions enjoyable and almost fun. And by making transitions enjoyable, they prevent behavior problems.

Organizing and Planning Activities

Scheduling and transition rituals have to do with helping children organize time. But there is more to planning a schedule than helping children organize time. There is also a need to help children sustain their directed activities within each block of time. As discussed in Chapter 8, this need involves developing a curriculum. However, it also involves planning for the curriculum to run well, as the following example illustrates:

> One day, an observer learned why the play with Legos always seemed go well in Sue's classroom, even though many of the boys involved could be behavior problems. Usually, when the boys complained about not having enough Legos, they were referring not to just any Legos but to the long blue ones that were key to their production process. But just before complaints turned into fights, Sue, the head teacher, always came up with a new supply of long blue Legos. She kept her own supply hidden for times of emergency. If she simply had put the blue Legos out all the time, one or two children might have hoarded them. This way, she maintained control over the distribution and, in the process, helped the children to maintain control over themselves.

The example above shows how behavior problems can be prevented through good planning around materials. In Chapter 8, we saw how developmental educators used clay as part of the curriculum to help children with behavior problems. In the next example, because of poor planning around materials, use of the same medium yielded far less successful results, which were symptomatic of poor programming in general in this particular classroom:

> During one of their demonstrations, the art educators introduced clay, a material that the children had never before used in the classroom (the teachers considered clay to be "too messy"). Unfortunately, during this demonstration, there had not been much thought given to the texture of the clay. Initially, the clay was too hard, but then, after adding too much water, it became too soft. Soon, the mushy clay was everywhere and everything was a mess. In terms of the project's goal of challenging teachers' values and practices, this demonstration was a nightmare. Messing with watery clay gave the teachers an excuse to interrupt the session. Children were told to hold their hands together and walk in a direct line to the bathroom while being careful not to touch anything—hardly what the project was designed to accomplish.

This one incident of poor planning did not in itself lead to behavior problems. However, repeated occurrences of this type of poor planning did prevent teachers from developing the kind of classroom where the curriculum worked to give children a voice. So, in this classroom, there were many children who remained somewhat isolated throughout the year.

In the next example, teachers planned for children to be able to paint, but their planning did not include ways to prevent the all too common scene that ensued:

> Susanne, a somewhat irritable and bossy child, enjoyed painting; when occupied with paints, she became much more agreeable and cooperative. On this day, the morning had not gone well, so Susanne seemed especially in need of painting. For the first five minutes, she painted intensely. But just before finishing, the yellow line at the top of her painting began to drip. Slowly, the drip made its way down the

center, running right through each of the figures she had drawn. Apparently, a teacher had not mixed the paints properly. The result was lots of screaming, tearing of paper, and tears.

As Carole Weinstein (1987, p. 163) observed, "A glue bottle that is clogged, paint that is too thin, or a puzzle with a piece missing make the completion of a task frustrating, if not impossible." And too much frustration can cause behavior problems:

In one class, the children were enthusiastically participating in making a quilt. The teachers seemed to have planned well. Each child seemed to have all the necessary tools and materials. However, when it came time for the children to cut out their pieces of cloth, they were handed children's scissors, which could not cut the cloth. The result was a good deal of frustration leading to children getting up, wandering away, and becoming disruptive.

Matching Activities to Children's Abilities

In our final example pertaining to programming, we show yet another way in which planning relates to the prevention of behavior problems. In this example, the importance of planning activities with children's abilities in mind is underscored through a demonstration of what can happen when there is a mismatch:

In one classroom, the art teacher came twice a week to lead projects with the children. One day, the project was to make dinosaurs from a series of paper plates. This involved painting, tracing, cutting, punching holes, and stapling. It was simply too difficult for the children because they were not skilled with scissors and tracing and because they could not use the stapler. To complete this project, each child needed a teacher's help. But there were only three teachers, counting the art teacher. As they waited for help, many of the children became bored and agitated. One little boy began flicking paint, and soon thereafter a paint fight broke out.

In sum, good programming goes a long way toward preventing behavior problems, and bad programming can be a definite cause of behavior problems. Teachers need to keep this in mind as they plan the course of a classroom's day.

Physical Environment

We begin this section on the built environment with an illustration of the relationship between physical environment—in this case, the arrangement of space—and children's problem behavior.

> As a visitor entered the classroom, three boys were at the far end poised as if to take off, and take off they did. Barreling down the middle of the classroom, they seemed like race car drivers at some small, local track. And like race car drivers, they did not stop at the end of the straightaway but rather continued on to make a curve, then headed back along the far edge of the classroom. Now they were no longer race car drivers. They had become runners competing in the high hurdles as they vaulted the two low risers dividing the far wall into activity areas. Once over the second riser, they again turned to make another run, but at that moment the head teacher screamed.

This is not an example of bad boys being bad. This is an example of children loving to run and taking a long open space in the middle of the classroom as an invitation to run.

In examining the physical environment and how it can cause behavior problems, we again focus on ways to provide ego support. As with the discussion on programming, providing ego support means minimizing frustrations and maximizing children's ability to orient themselves. The frustrations involve continually having to exert self-control in the face of temptations provided by the way the physical environment is built. And the frustrations have to do with annoyances caused by the built environment, for example, children bumping into one another when there is not enough space. Orientation has to do with children locating themselves in space so that they are aware of where they are, where they can go, and how they should act accordingly.

We concentrate on four topics in particular. The first is the overall architectural plan of a classroom or center and whether the plan is open, closed, or modified open. Here, we consider the nature of a classroom's activity pockets and pathways. The second topic is meeting areas and whether they are designed for comfort, ease of looking, and room to prevent poking and nudging. The third topic is storage areas and systems for retrieving materials and returning them to their proper places. The fourth topic is private places where children can retreat in order to be alone or away from adults.

Types of Architectural Plans

Gary Moore is an architect as well as a developmental psychologist who studies the effects of different architectural plans for early childhood centers (Moore, 1987). He began his research by describing three different kinds of plans. The first, called an open plan, is distinguished by the presence of open spaces without partitions. The classroom in the previous example followed an open plan. The second, called a closed plan, is distinguished by self-contained classrooms or separate rooms for separate kinds of activities. The third, called a modified open plan, is distinguished by the variety of small and large activity spaces that are open enough to allow children to see the play possibilities available to them yet provide enough enclosure for the children to be protected from noise and visual distraction. According to Moore, of the three, the modified open plan best meets the needs of children. Moreover, the plan is the best in ways relevant to our subject of behavior problems.

The key to understanding why modified open plans prevent or minimize behavior problems has to do with what promotes children's constructive initiative. Moore showed that compared to the closed plan, open and modified open plans promote the ability of children to act on their own initiative. But the initiative taken by

children in centers following an open plan is often of the type illustrated in the opening example: random or inappropriate activity
that requires teachers to step in and take control. In contrast, the
initiative taken by children in centers following a modified open
plan is often constructive exploration and play that allows children
to take control and allows teachers to support them.

That a modified open plan promotes more constructive exploration and play is not surprising. In classrooms following such a
plan, children are faced with a variety of well-defined activity
pockets—places that seemingly cry out for children to use them in
well-defined and constructive ways. Furthermore, these activity
pockets are clearly bounded, that is, separated from circulation space
and from other activity pockets, and, typically, they accommodate
groups of three or four children, the group size where young children often function at their social best.

Modified open centers also have circulation paths that flow
through the classroom, overlooking and connecting activity pockets but not cutting through them. Often, these circulation paths are
meandering as they weave around furniture and partitions designed
to prevent running. Our earlier example from an open plan classroom illustrates what can happen when circulation paths are
straight, not meandering; here is an example of what can happen
when a circulation path comes too close to an activity area:

In one very small classroom, there were really only two places that
children could go to play and construct: a table in the center of the
classroom and a small rug in the corner. Because the table was at
the center of the room, it was a place where the children were often
interrupted. For example, on one occasion, half the class was at the
table working on an art project. They were continually interrupted by
the other children, who were carrying bins of toy cars from one side
of the room to the other. There was not enough room for the children
with the cars to pass the table without interfering, and their interfer-
ence caused considerable commotion among all of the children.

In sum, with the modified open plan, unlike the open and closed plans, the variety and definition of spaces as well as the connections between the spaces give children numerous options for initiating constructive exploration and play.

Meeting Areas

The meeting area is typically a hotbed for behavior problems because there young children have to do things that they are not very good at, such as sitting, waiting, listening, and being next to other children without nudging or poking them. It is crucial, therefore, that meeting areas be well designed. Here is one early childhood teacher's recollection of redesigning a meeting area to reduce the frequency of behavior problems:

> The previous meeting area consisted of hard, wooden benches located in what is now the block area. Meeting times were very difficult for both children and teachers. On the stiff benches, children squirmed a lot. And the fact that the benches allowed the children to observe a group in another classroom did not help. The newer meeting area is located in a protected corner, which focuses children's attention on the teacher in front of them. The riser-style seats are made of plywood covered with carpet. Now, the children have plenty of support, and there is much less squirming and looking about.

This example indicates that softness for sitting and control of children's lines of vision are two important aspects of well-designed meeting areas. For some teachers, providing boundaries between children is another, whether achieved by carpet squares for sitting, tape, or, for children with serious problems respecting boundaries, chairs. In sum, well-designed meeting areas offer spaces in which children have comfortable places to sit, areas where they can easily focus their attention on the teacher without distractions, and where there is help for them to respect boundaries and keep their bodies from touching others.

Storage Areas and Storage Systems

Developmental education is often criticized for not offering children enough structure or direction. What critics usually mean is that developmental education does not lead teachers to do all of the directing. But this criticism overlooks the fact that in good developmental classrooms, even though teachers are not always telling children what they should or should not do, there is a lot of structure and directing. The structure and directing are simply of a different type. The way in which materials are stored is an illuminating case in point.

In a good developmental classroom, we are likely to see shelves within children's reach that are stocked with all kinds of materials, organized in such a way that each piece of equipment and each type of material has its own special place. Even the art supplies will be sorted, with markers, paper, scissors, crayons, and the rest having their own, distinctive place—in contrast to a giant plastic container with everything thrown in and jumbled together. Without a word spoken, the message is "Please use the equipment and materials if you wish, but take care of them and return them to their proper place." That is structure. Storage areas and storage systems thus play an important role in stimulating constructive initiative and responsible behavior and in promoting the ideal of a classroom as a "busy beehive."

Unfortunately, in many classrooms for young children, equipment and materials are either missing, kept out of reach of children, or organized in such a way that children cannot easily find what they want and need. The result is either children not finding enough to do or teachers having to assume too much control. The following examples illustrate:

In one classroom for four year olds, the head teacher spoke of showing his children "tough love." What he actually showed them was an authoritarian style that stifled initiative and prevented behavior problems from ever becoming opportunities to learn. His style was nowhere more clearly expressed than in the way equipment and materials were stored: behind a black curtain where children were forbidden to go. He was the sole dispenser of equipment and materials. It was his initiative, not the children's, that made this classroom go. As a result, there was order at the expense of children never learning self-control. This became apparent on days when he was absent. On those days, the children became wild and were often completely out of control.

In another classroom for four year olds, children could access equipment and materials, but the way in which they were stored on shelves made it difficult for them to do so. Art supplies were thrown together, as were all kinds of construction materials. Even the unit blocks had no clear spots marking where they should go. As a result, children in this classroom took less initiative than one would have liked and less responsibility for returning equipment and materials to their proper places. They too became overly dependent on teachers' suggestions for what they should do.

These two examples entail different problems in the way equipment and materials were stored, but they share the same outcome: the children did not take enough initiative to involve themselves in constructive things to do.

Places for Retreats

Places for children to retreat and have privacy or time away from adults can be instrumental in helping children "cool out" and thereby in preventing behavior problems. The following example clarifies this point:

The classroom had a loft area, a wonderfully realistic two-story house, complete with roof, walls, and Plexiglas windows. The children used this loft as a retreat area, but the place was not without problems. The fact that it was so enclosed meant it was inaccessible to teachers, thus unmonitored, and isolating for children. This invited skirmishes within and occasional missiles directed at the group below.

The classroom itself was one long, large corridor with high ceilings. It was full of materials and places to sit and work, but it had no good place for retreat, no place for a child to be alone but not isolated. Even the book nook was in the middle of the classroom and susceptible to traffic and interruptions.

So, the teachers began to redesign the loft area to better meet the needs of the children. They created what came to be known as "the cave," a place where children could go when they wanted to be alone but a place where they and the teachers could still feel connected. First, they removed the walls and made the space more open, with a guard rail for safety. Then, to create the cave, we placed several slender wooden slats diagonally and vertically from the outside ceiling of the cave to the floor. The children and teachers brought in threads, ribbons, and other materials to weave between and around the slats so as to give a spider-web appearance. Inside, they covered the foam walls and ceiling with black velvet and filled the cave with large pillows covered with a brightly patterned fabric. The black created the feeling of being in a cave while the wooden slats and weaving created interesting light patterns within the area. Most important, teachers could see into the cave even while children within felt they had privacy and could not be seen.

The children were immediately drawn to the cave. They brought in books and blankets and settled in to relax, "cool out," and reenergize. Furthermore, they began to remove themselves to the cave just at those times when they were about to lose control and get out of hand. Unlike the time-out bench, the cave became a neutral territory for regrouping. If, for example, a child was about to lose self-control in group meeting, he or she was allowed to go quietly to the cave until ready to rejoin the group. Some days it took five minutes to regroup, other days it took longer, but always the child emerged in control and ready to participate.

Summary and Conclusion

In this chapter, we have examined how programming and the physical environment can play a role in managing and preventing behavior problems. And, once again, we see that control need not reside in an authoritarian rule by the teacher. When teachers do a good job controlling programming and the physical environment, they promote children's self-control. When they do not, they elicit behavior problems.

All this is "old hat" to experienced early childhood educators, but it bears repeating, nonetheless, because what is old can sometimes get lost in discussions focusing too much on what is relatively new. It also bears repeating because a good many who make decisions about the design of environments for children do not have the wisdom and expertise of experienced teachers. We are reminded of a local hospital that recently spent a good deal of money redesigning its pediatric outpatient clinic, resulting in an enormous reception desk being placed in the middle of what used to be play space—thus ensuring that visiting children would have a harder, not easier, time adapting to the hospital environment. The design team for that hospital could have used a good early childhood educator.

Part Four

· ·

Behavior Problems and Diversity

We are all more similar than otherwise.
            Harry Stack Sullivan (1953, p. xviii)

In Part Four, we explore the three most common sources of diversity associated with behavior problems: children from minority cultures, children with chronic and serious behavior problems, and children with special needs. All three sources put children at risk for mistreatment by teachers when behavior control and management constitute the teachers' overall aim. Further, all three put children at risk for being labeled deficient when, in fact, they have strengths and age-appropriate needs. We must accommodate children's strengths and needs and, in the process, keep their development as our overall aim.

10

Culture and Behavior Problems

The Language of Control

Cynthia Ballenger

This chapter is a revised and abbreviated version of a 1992 article appearing in Harvard Educational Review. *Here, Cynthia Ballenger seems to challenge our developmental approach by showing us the limitations of overvaluing what we have called educational management and prevention tactics. At first glance, she seems to imply that we should be more controlling and not be so afraid or reluctant to call some behavior bad. In this respect, she is telling us the same thing that some Haitian parents and teachers have told us: in the process of bending over backwards to be supportive, we are actually letting children "get away with murder," to their own detriment and ours.*

But there is another, different lesson to draw from this wonderful work on culture and behavior problems, namely, that different cultures have different ideas of what development is all about. The dominant culture of North America shields children from thinking too much about adult responsibility while they cultivate their special interests and abilities during childhood. Then, at the end of adolescence, we expect individuals to be mature, to move away from this protective cocoon, to stay in touch by telephone, mail, an occasional visit, and so on, and to strike out on their own. We take it for granted, then, that development is a process of growing up and away, a process that leaves children obligated only to become "the best they can be" as they become what they want to be. Beyond this, they owe little to others.

This picture of development is not shared by all cultures. Other cultures emphasize not individuality and responsibility coming from freedom but rather interdependence and responsibility coming from obligation. Other cultures find it strange that we see interdependence and obligation in such negative, even oppressive terms because, to them, feeling obligated to one's family and (often) to one's God is both natural and necessary. Their picture of development, then, is about becoming aware of the interdependence and obligations inherent to their most important connections.

But notice how we keep revisiting this theme of connection, regardless of differences in cultural heritage and worldview. For in the end, every culture, ours included, wants its children to feel connected in deep and lasting ways. One central theme of this book is that feeling connected is the soil where good behavior grows and where children begin to develop self-control. In other words, in the end, cross-cultural differences turn out to be simply differences in means to a common end.

W. George Scarlett

This chapter is the result of a year spent in conversations about teaching, difficult conversations in which I, a seasoned teacher and fledgling sociolinguist, was only rarely the informed party. Some of these conversations occurred with public school teachers and academic researchers who were attempting to develop a common language and a shared set of values with which to approach classroom issues. Others took place in an evening course I cotaught, a course for Haitian adults who wished to teach in day care. And still others happened in the preschool where I was teaching during the day, a preschool serving primarily the children of Haitian immigrants. All of these conversations focused on questions about teaching Haitian children.

For many years, I questioned whether Haitian children were getting what they needed in the average North American preschool. In my previous work, I had noticed that, increasingly, Haitian children were being referred to my class for children with special needs. As these children arrived at my class, they were accompanied by all kinds of concerns from educational professionals: they were "wild," they had "no language," their mothers were "depressed." Some of the children I saw did indeed have genuine problems, and yet, time and again, I found that after a period of adjustment, they were responsive, intelligent children; their mothers were perhaps homesick and unhappy in a strange, cold country, but generally they were not clinically depressed.

During that period of questioning, I came to understand that in order to see the children more clearly, I would need to learn the Haitian language and to study Haitian culture. After a period at graduate school studying sociolinguistics, I took a position as a preschool teacher in a bilingual school where both Haitian Creole and English were spoken and where Haitian culture was central. I was the only teacher at that school who was not Haitian, and, although by that time I spoke Creole, I was still getting to know the culture. As a graduate student in sociolinguistics, I had done research; as a teacher, I had thought about teaching; I was now involved in trying to approach issues as a teacher-researcher. The work that I report on here was part of many conversations. My goal is to present some of the different voices that I heard in the course of those conversations and to discuss the process I went through in learning to control a class of four-year-old Haitian children.

Problems

Having had many years of experience teaching in early childhood programs, I did not expect to have problems when I came to the Haitian preschool. However, I did. The children ran me ragged. In the friendliest, most cheerful, and affectionate manner imaginable, my class of four year olds followed their own inclinations rather than my directions. Although I claim to be a person who does not need to have a great deal of control, in this case I had very little and I did not like it.

My frustration increased when I looked at the other classrooms. I noticed that the other teachers, all Haitian women, had orderly classrooms of children who, in an equally affectionate and cheerful manner, *did* follow directions. In these other classrooms, the teachers kept the confusion to a level I could well have tolerated. I was forced to admit that the overriding problem resided not in the children but in the mismatch between my teaching and the children.

I took my observations to the group of Haitian preschool teachers whom I was teaching in the child development course. They quickly recognized the problem in their own terms. As part of the course, they were all interning in various day-care centers, some with me at the Haitian school, the majority in other centers. Several of the teachers in the other centers were extremely concerned about behavior problems. What they told me was that many of the children in their centers were behaving very poorly. They felt that this was particularly true of the Haitian children. They felt that the way in which they were being instructed as teachers to deal with the children's problem behavior was not effective. One woman related that when she was hit by a four year old, she was instructed to acknowledge, first, the anger the child must be feeling and then to explain to him that he could not hit. She told me that from her point of view this approach was the same as saying, "Why don't you hit me again?"

When I talked with Haitian parents at my school, I again heard similar complaints. From their points of view, the behavior tolerated in their neighborhood schools was disrespectful; the children were *allowed* to misbehave. A common refrain in these conversations was, "We're losing a generation of children," that is, the young children here now, who were not being raised in Haiti. However, when I asked for specific advice about things I might do to manage the children better, the teachers and parents were at a loss for suggestions.

So, I took my problem to the Brookline Teacher-Researcher Seminar (BTRS). The members of BTRS had come to share a focus on language, or rather the diversity of languages, that one finds in schools: the language of instruction, the language of children, the language of science, and so on. Thus, in our conversations, the BTRS group encouraged me to approach my problem by discovering what it was that the Haitian teachers *said* to the children in situations where directions were given and where the language was about control.

With this encouragement, I began to write down what the Haitian teachers said to the children in situations where the children's behavior was at issue. I then brought these transcribed texts to the various conversations in which I participated: with the Haitian teachers in the child development course, with the North American teachers in BTRS, and with the parents and teachers at the school where I was teaching. I present here fragments of these Haitian teacher-student texts that I consider typical in form and content, and then I share some of the responses and the thinking engendered by these texts among the people with whom I had been conversing.

The first text sample is from Clothilde's account of an event at her day-care center. Clothilde is a middle-age Haitian woman and a student in the child development course. She has a great deal of experience with children, both from raising her own and from caring for other people's, and many of her classmates turn to her for advice. During a conversation in our group, she complained about the behavior of the Haitian children in the day-care center where she taught. She felt that the North American teachers were not controlling the children adequately.

One day, Clothilde experienced a defining moment on the matter of children's problem behavior. As she arrived at her school, she watched a teacher telling a little Haitian child that the child needed to go into her classroom, that she could not stay alone in the hall. The child refused and eventually kicked the teacher. Clothilde had had enough. She asked the director to bring her all the Haitian children right away. The director and Clothilde gathered the children into the large common room. The following is the text of what she told me she said to the children:

CLOTHILDE: Does your mother let you bite?
CHILDREN: No.
CLOTHILDE: Does your father let you punch kids?
CHILDREN: No.
CLOTHILDE: Do you kick at home?
CHILDREN: No.
CLOTHILDE: You don't respect anyone, not the teachers who play with you or the adults who work upstairs. You need to respect adults, even people you see on the streets. You are taking good ways you learn at home and not bringing them to school. You're taking the bad things you learn at school and taking them home. You're not going to do this anymore. Do you want your parents to be ashamed of you?

According to Clothilde, the Haitian children have been well-behaved ever since. Other Haitian teachers with whom I have shared this text have confirmed that that was what the children needed to hear. However, they also said that Clothilde will have to repeat her speech because the children will not remain well-behaved indefinitely without a reminder.

The next text involves an event at my school. Josiane, who has taught for many years both in the United States and in Haiti, was reprimanding a group of children who had been making a lot of noise while their teacher was trying to give them directions:

JOSIANE: When your mother talks to you, don't you listen?
CHILDREN: Yes.
JOSIANE: When your mother says, "Go get something," don't you go get it?
CHILDREN: Yes.
JOSIANE: When your mother says, "Go to the bathroom," don't you go?
CHILDREN: Yes.
JOSIANE: You know why I'm telling you this. Because I want you to be good children. When an adult talks to you, you're supposed to listen so you will become a good person. The adults here like you, they want you to become good children.

Finally, here is Jeremie's father speaking to him. Jeremie is a very active four year old, and the staff had asked his father to help them in controlling his behavior:

FATHER: Are you going to be good? (Jeremie nods at each pause.) Are you going to listen to Miss Cindy? Are you going to listen to Miss Josiane? Because they like you. They love you. Do it for me. Do it for God. God loves you.

Reflections

The content and the form of these texts are different from what I and many other North American teachers would probably have produced in the same circumstances. I shared these and other texts and observations with many parents and teachers, both Haitian and North American. I asked them to reflect with me on how these conversations were different and what underpinned them. In this section, I present a blend of many people's observations and self-reflections, including my own.

The Haitian preschool teachers had clear insights about the behavior of North American teachers. Clothilde commented that in her experience North American teachers frequently refer to children's internal states and interpret their feelings for them: "You must be angry," "It's hard for you when your friend does that," and so on. Clothilde pointed out that in her speech she never refers to children's emotions; other Haitian teachers I have observed also do not do this as a rule.

Rose, another Haitian teacher, also commented that North American teachers often refer to specific factors in a child's situation that, in the teachers' opinions, may have influenced the child's behavior. For example, the teachers of Michel, a boy whose mother had abandoned him, often told him that they understood that he missed his mother, but that regarding his toys, he nevertheless needed to share. When a child pushes or pinches another child sitting next to him or her, many North American teachers will suggest that if the child does not like people to sit so close, he or she should say so rather than pinch. Rose believed, and, based on my observations, I concur, that Haitian teachers rarely do this. Josiane suggested further that if she was concerned about an individual child and his or her particular problems, instead of articulating them for the child, her goal would be "to make the child feel comfortable with the group." If the child were misbehaving, she believed that she would say, "You know I'm your friend," and then she would remind the child that "We don't do that." In fact, I have seen her do exactly that many times—and with excellent results.

These examples suggest to me a difference in focus between the North American and Haitian teachers. It seems that North American teachers characteristically are concerned with articulating for a child his or her feelings and problems. In contrast, Clothilde, Josiane, and other Haitian people whom I spoke with and observed are concerned with articulating for a child his or her connections to those who care for the child: parents, teachers, God, and so on.

Of course, both North American and Haitian teachers refer to the family, but in different ways. North American teachers are likely to mention particular characteristics of a child's family, characteristics that are specific to that family and are seen as perhaps responsible for the child's behavior, or misbehavior. In contrast, Haitian teachers are likely to refer to what families have in common. Families do not differ in their desire that children respect adults, that children behave properly, and that children do not shame them. Therefore, by speaking in unison, as in Clothilde's and Josiane's texts above, the children's answers present a vivid enactment of the sort of unity that the Haitian teachers' approach seeks to engender.

Another difference in approach to problem behavior that the Haitian teachers noted is the use of consequences. North American teachers typically present the particular consequences of an act of misbehavior. For example, I often say things like "He's crying because you hit him" or "If you don't listen to me, you won't know what to do." Haitian teachers are less likely to differentiate among particular kinds of misbehavior; they condemn them all as examples of "bad" behavior. Clothilde is typical of the Haitian teachers in that the immediate consequences are not made explicit; she does not explain why she is against biting or punching. She instead refers to such behavior as "bad," and then she explains to the children the consequences of bad behavior in general, such as shame for the family. Jeremie's father simply tells him to be good, to be good for those who love him. Josiane, too, tells the children to be good because the people who like them want them to be good. I have heard other Haitian teachers refer to the impression that bad behavior would create in a passer-by, or to the necessity of modeling good behavior for younger children. But Haitian teachers rarely mention the specific consequences of particular acts, a clear difference from the speech of North American teachers.

In the Haitian texts, one has the impression that the children share the adults' understanding of what constitutes bad behavior. Clothilde's series of rhetorical questions—"Does your mother let you bite?" "Does your father let you punch kids?" and so on—is an example of the frame that many Haitian teachers adopt when addressing children about their behavior. The children understand their role without difficulty; they repeat the expected answers in choral unison. The choice of this format, that is, questions to which the answers are already known, emphasizes the fact that the children already know that their behavior is wrong.

In contrast, in the North American control situation, children often appear to be receiving new information. If there is a consensus about certain behavior being bad and other behavior good, North American teachers don't present it this way. Rather, they explain the consequences of particular actions as if they are trying to convince or teach the children that there is a problem with their behavior. As presented in school, misbehavior is considered wrong not because of anything inherent to it but because of its particular consequences or perhaps because the behavior stems from feelings that the children have failed to identify and control.

These differences in approach to problem behavior between Haitian and North American teachers, as I came to recognize and understand them, seemed significant enough to account for some of the difficulties I had been experiencing in my classroom. But what to do about them?

Practice

With the overwhelming evidence that the Haitian children in my care were used to a kind of control talk other than what I had been providing, I have since adopted aspects of the style of Haitian teachers. I assume that I am not very good at it, that I have no idea of the nuances, and that I continue to follow many of the ways in which I have tried to manage behavior in the past. Nevertheless, I have developed a more or less stable melange of styles, and my control in the classroom has improved significantly. In addition, I find that I love trying out this Haitian way.

One of my recent experiences continues to resonate. I was reprimanding a boy for pinching another. In the Haitian manner, I was focusing on his prior, indisputable knowledge that pinching was simply no good. I also used my best approximation of the facial expression and tone of voice that I have seen and heard the Haitian teachers use in encounters of this kind. I can tell when I have it more or less right because of the way the children pay attention. As I finished talking, the other children, who had been rapt, all solemnly thanked me. They were perhaps feeling in danger of being pinched and felt that I had at last been effective. This solemn sort of response, which has occurred a few other times, gives me the sense that these situations of dealing with problem behavior are very important to them.

The following exchange suggests more about the way in which these efforts at managing misbehavior are important to the children. Recently, I was angrily reprimanding the children about their failure to wait for me while crossing a parking lot:

CYNTHIA: Did I tell you to go?
CHILDREN: No.
CYNTHIA: Can you cross this parking lot by yourselves?
CHILDREN: No.
CYNTHIA: That's right. There are cars here. They are dangerous. I don't want you to go alone. Why do I want you to wait for me, do you know?
CLAUDETTE: Yes. Because you like us.

Although I was following the usual Haitian frame of rhetorical questions with "no" answers, I had been expecting a final response based on the North American system of cause and effect, something like, "Because the cars are dangerous." Claudette, however, although she understands perfectly well the danger cars present to small children, did not expect to use that information in this kind of an interaction. What, then, was she telling me? Perhaps the same thing that the solemn children also meant in the earlier-cited incident, that there is intimacy and caring in this kind of talk. This is certainly the feeling I get from these experiences. I feel especially connected to the children in those instances in which I seem to have gotten it right.

Larger Context

North American teachers generally think of reprimands as put-downs, particularly when they are directed toward young children who are just learning to control their behavior. With this thinking, North Americans are reluctant to reprimand and will take great pains to avoid saying "No" or "Don't." However, I have learned from working with Haitian teachers and Haitian children that there are situations in which reprimands can both confirm and strengthen relationships and, in a sense, can define relationships for the child, as seems to have been the case for Claudette in the example above.

These opportunities to strengthen relationships with certain children may be lost when we go to great lengths to avoid actually telling children that they are wrong and that we disagree or disapprove. When we look at the differences between the ways in which things are done at home and at school, and the negative consequences that may emerge from these mismatches for children with minority cultural backgrounds, the area of problem behavior and the way it is responded to are particularly important because they directly affect the nature of the relationship between teacher and child because managing problem behavior well develops trust and mismanaging does the opposite.

When I began this project, I was aware that this subject of reprimands is a hotbed of disagreement: North Americans often perceive Haitians as too severe, both verbally and in their use of physical punishment, while Haitians often perceive North Americans as allowing children to become extraordinarily fresh and out of control. As members of a minority community, Haitian immigrant parents are at once ashamed and defiantly supportive of their community's disciplinary standards and methods.

In order to better represent the views of Haitians with whom I had spoken, I asked them to reflect again on our two cultures after they had heard my interpretations. People, of course, offered many varied points of view, yet everybody emphasized a sense of having grown up very "protected" in Haiti, of having been safe there both from involvement in serious trouble and from harm. This sense of being protected was largely based on their understanding that their entire extended family as well as many people in the community were involved in their upbringing. Some pointed out that Haitian families in the United States are smaller and less extended. United States Haitian communities, while tight in many ways, generally are more loosely connected than in Haiti.

This change in social structure was bemoaned by the people with whom I spoke, especially with regard to bringing up children. They attributed to this change their sense that this generation of children, particularly those born in the United States, is increasingly at risk. They are at risk not only of losing connection to their parents' culture but also, and as a consequence, of falling prey to the drugs, crime, and other problems of urban life.

Yet, everyone I spoke with also recalled some pain in their growing up, pain they relate to the respect and obedience they were required to exhibit to all adults, which at times conflicted with their own developing desire to express their opinions and make their own choices. However, this pain was not to be discarded lightly. For many of the Haitian people with whom I spoke, religious values underpinned the twin issues of respect and obedience; in some ways, respect for and obedience to parents and other adults reflect respect for and obedience to God.

Many people seemed to agree with the ambivalence expressed by one Haitian mother, a lawyer, who told me that while she had suffered as a child because of the uncompromising respect and obedience demanded of her in her family, she continued to see respect and obedience as values she needed to impart to her children. She was one of many Haitians who told me of instances where a child from a poor family, a child with neither clothes nor supplies for school, had succeeded eventually in becoming a doctor or a lawyer. In these accounts, as in her own case, it is in large measure the strictness of the family that is regarded as the source of the child's accomplishment rather than the talent or the power of the individual.

Presumably, there are varying degrees of tension in all societies between individual and community, and presumably this tension is best preserved, not undone. The accounts I have shared suggest the form this tension often takes within Haitian culture. I am, however, struck and troubled by the powerful individualism and relative lack of tension underlying the approach identified here as characteristic of North American teachers. It appears that North Americans speak as if enlightened self-interest were the ultimate moral guideline. In comparison to the language used by the Haitian teachers, North American teachers' language seems to place very little emphasis on shared values and a moral community.

Conclusion

The process of gaining multicultural understanding in education must be dual in nature. On the one hand, cultural behavior that at first seems strange and inexplicable should become familiar; on the other hand, one's own familiar values and practices should become at least temporarily strange and subject to examination. In addition to the information I have gained that helps me to manage and form relationships with Haitian children in my classroom, I also value greatly the extent to which these conversations, by forcing me to empathize with and understand a view of the world that is in many ways very different from my own, have led me to reexamine values and principles that had become inaccessible under layers of assumptions.

Currently, I am not teaching Haitian children, although I continue to visit those who were in my preschool class. In my next round of teaching, I expect to have a classroom with children from a wide range of backgrounds. It is difficult to say how my last experience will illuminate the next, or, analogously, how my experience can be of use to teachers in different kinds of classrooms. I do believe that teachers need to try to examine and understand both their own assumptions and the culturally constituted meanings that children from all backgrounds bring to school. It seems to me that accommodation must be made on all sides so that no group has to abandon the ways in which it is accustomed to passing on its values. I was fortunate to have access to the knowledge and collaboration of so many people, Haitian and North American, to help me begin to understand my own experience. All of these conversations have been rewarding. I have made new friends and, I believe, become a better teacher.

11

When Kindergartners Don't Act in Kindergarten Ways

Monique Jette

Children being "ready" for kindergarten is a concern in many schools. But this notion of readiness suggests that teachers should not have to teach to children at different levels of maturity. In this chapter, we see a different attitude and approach. We see Monique Jette and her coteachers making themselves more ready to teach to a diverse group. They did so by adjusting their teaching to meet the developmental needs of five children who were not acting in the usual kindergarten ways. We are reminded here of Kohlberg and Lickona's suggestion that "early childhood educators . . . need to think of themselves as experimenters trying out different strategies to determine which enable children to operate at the cutting edge of their developmental capacity." Here, once again, diversity challenges the developmental approach. And here, once again, meeting the challenge shows the versatility of a developmental approach.

W. George Scarlett

After teaching in the classroom for four year olds at a university day-care center, I was excited about moving up to teach kindergarten. The other teachers I would join were both veterans.

Many of the children would be children I had taught the year before. And the environment would be wonderfully rich in opportunities for children to learn. I looked forward to implementing a new curriculum and supporting the development of five year olds.

Once the year began, my excitement continued. The first months of school were filled with productive activity, and, with each passing day, it was clear that most of the twenty-four children felt empowered by their new identity as kindergartners and proud to act in kindergarten ways. We teachers had reason to feel good.

However, five children were neither feeling empowered nor acting in kindergarten ways. In particular, these five lacked skills and motivation to form cooperative relationships. At the time, we were aware of their problems but not overly concerned. We saw them as adjusting at their own pace. Besides, at that time, their behavior did not affect the class as a whole.

During our first days together, our goals were to foster a feeling of community and to teach the children how they could take advantage of what the class had to offer. We began by teaching ways to use the many learning areas spread throughout the classroom. We articulated rules for using the areas: for limiting the number of children allowed in each, for defining appropriate use of materials, for establishing procedures for cleaning up, and so on. We stressed that this classroom belonged to everyone and that everyone was to take care of it. When children became skilled at using the areas constructively, we pointed this out. When they had problems, we gave them help.

Also, to reach our goals, we helped children settle into a daily routine. We carefully balanced structured activity with free play. We provided a comfortable mix of familiar activity times with unfamiliar writing and math workshops. Children responded well to the new, more academic times and expressed pride in being kindergartners.

We also did much to get close to children, to create bonds we knew would help children feel secure and that would motivate them to learn and grow. Each teacher did so in his or her own way. My way was through active play, especially outside play: chase games and dramatic play with lots of running, physical activity, and fantasy roles. In contrast, Kristen, another teacher, took a more nurturing approach. For example, she often sought out children to scoop them into her lap and then engage them in tickling games and gentle roughhousing.

At the time, we truly believed our children were coming together as a group. Now, upon reflection, we realize the five children referred to previously were not really with us. Our seeing these children as adjusting "at their own pace" denied the seriousness of their problems, problems we eventually had to face when these children began to disrupt the classroom and impose their own, *un*kindergartenlike ways.

All five of these children came from homes experiencing serious family problems, problems that were not of the children's making and over which they had little control. To a great extent, their behavior problems were expressions of these family problems. These five also shared with one another a propensity for "losing it," for engaging in tantrums when they did not get their way, for opposing adults, and for being moody.

However, despite these similarities, each child was different and special in his or her own way. Barry was active and outgoing but lacked the play skills to sustain cooperative play. Matthew had plenty of skills but showed an intimidating toughness that kept children away. Cathy was lively and dramatic, but sometimes she confused fantasy with reality. Todd showed a lot of play skills when alone but too often remained alone. Finally, Max had a lot of energy and enthusiasm but often became impulsive and disorganized.

The problems of these five began to infect the entire classroom. They made activity periods increasingly difficult to manage. They caused children to spend extra amounts of time in unfocused, unproductive play. Group meetings became particularly dreaded by all. With such a large group, we expected some disruption: our share of children arguing, poking, and calling out in disruptive ways. During the first months, we managed these disruptions through group problem solving and by reminding children of the rules. However, over time, our efforts to manage failed as meetings degenerated and as the group became wildly out of control.

The turn downward led us to question why so much was going wrong when all had seemed to be going right. Was our developmental approach to guiding children and managing their behavior problems good for some but not all? When teaching children with serious behavior problems, should we switch to a different, less developmental approach? At that point, we thought the answer to both questions was yes. So, with the five children whom we by then saw as major instigators of classroom disorder, we revised our approach. With them, we instituted purely behavior tactics designed to control. For example, we instituted behavior charts that made limits clear and consequences certain.

However, our behavior tactics were not enough. We felt pulled in too many directions as these five demanded so much individual attention while we still had a complicated program to run. So, after several team meetings, we decided to experiment and work with these five in a separate room for a few hours each day.

This decision ran counter to the center's practice of including all children in regular classrooms. At the time, then, the decision seemed a double betrayal: first, a betrayal of our commitment to developmental education and, second, a betrayal of our commitment to inclusion. But the small group experiment proved to be anything but a betrayal. Rather, it expanded our understanding of what constitutes a developmental approach, and it served as another tool for inclusion.

Through their behavior problems, the five children had been telling us that we were not developmental enough: we were not addressing their needs to work on younger issues before tackling kindergarten issues. These five, then, were telling us to slow down, start over, and rebuild foundations necessary for acting in kindergarten ways. In particular, these children needed added supports to learn how to become members of a group who know how to play.

Small Group Experiment

Our building of psychological foundations was reflected in the way we built the small classroom from scratch. We began with a tiny, empty room. The group decided what the room would contain. Eagerly, the children chose their favorites: markers, Legos, Playdoh, books, and blocks. Teachers also made choices. We placed only one table in the room with enough seating for all. Using pillows from our classroom, we created a cozy corner. Also, to store personal items, we made each child a small cubbylike area. The room quickly had a homey feel and the look of an inviting learning space.

Next, we generated a list of "Our Rules." Each child contributed his or her own. It is noteworthy that the rules suggested by a child often reflected his or her behavior problems. So, Matthew, who often swore, suggested No Swearing; Cathy, who often engaged in tantrums, suggested No Throwing Things; and so forth. By suggesting these rules, the children showed both awareness of their problems and their need for help in managing those problems. In the end, we listed our rules on a huge chart, which everyone decorated and which we hung prominently on a wall throughout our stay.

It was this first experience in rule making that made us realize that the experiment was thoroughly developmental and consistent with our values. We were acting in the segregated group much as we would have acted in an integrated group, only with more focus and energy for these five children. And what we did here was obviously geared toward helping them fit into any group. By designing and constructing the room together, the children took a big step toward understanding the workings of groups, something they had missed before.

Maintaining the group's identity and dealing with disruptive behaviors in ways that promoted learning constituted our main task.

We were there, then, to foster learning and development, not just manage behavior problems. The following example illustrates our approach:

> One day, during the first week of our "special time," the group was preparing to go to the library to select books for our room. As the children gathered by the door, Matthew buried himself in a corner with pillows. He remained silent as Kristen gently encouraged him, saying, "Matthew, we need your help to pick out books." Kristen immediately recognized the opportunity to use Matthew's behavior as a learning experience for the group. The agenda changed from "We need to get books" to "What can we do to include Matthew?" Kristen announced, "We need to help Matthew right now before we can go for books. I wonder what Matthew may be thinking about, and I wonder what we can do to help Matthew be ready to go with us even though he's so sad." As Kristen spoke, Matthew clutched his pillows and pulled them tightly over his head.
>
> The other children were intrigued by Kristen's questions. One child responded, "Here, Matthew, you can hug my teddy bear if you want." And in a very nurturing, caring way, he placed the bear next to Matthew. Another child offered, "Maybe Matthew will feel better if he punches my Hulk Hogan pillow!" Matthew seemed to like this suggestion because he did, in fact, punch the pillow. And still another child suggested, "Maybe he needs time by hisself." After about ten minutes of discussion, Matthew stood up and announced, "I want to go to the library." The group then resumed its original agenda with full participation from all.

If we had been interested in controlling Matthew, we would likely have used a more behavioral approach. But we were not. Rather, we were most interested in creating a group and making it possible for each child to identify himself or herself as a member of the group.

This example also illustrates how a smaller group can provide support for children with strong desires to control, who feel threatened by even minor attempts to get them to cooperate. In the larger group, with the pushes and pulls of so many children, the curriculum, and a class schedule, it was difficult to help children such as Matthew see the benefits of giving up or sharing control. But in the smaller group, such benefits were clear.

The small group also offered more opportunities for interactive fantasy play and deep play, where children expressed and embedded troublesome feelings. In this play, the teachers acted as playmates. We followed their lead and took up roles in their dramas. Compared to the larger classroom, it was truly a luxury to be able to spend long periods of time in child-directed play. In this play, the children frequently created fantasies with important personal meanings. For example,

> When Todd imitated the actions and sounds of a kitten, and then nuzzled up beside Kristen, Kristen commented, "Oh, What's this? A cat?" In a quiet voice Todd responded, "I'm a baby kitten. You're the mommy cat." "Oh, come here my baby!" Kristen implored and gestured for Todd to be cradled in her lap. As he did this, Cathy became interested and imitated Todd's kitten behavior. Todd responded sharply, "No! This mommy has just one baby!" Cathy then remarked, "I want to be adopted because I don't have a mother!" Todd then asked, "Where is your father?" Very matter-of-factly, Cathy replied, "Oh, he's too busy to take care of me." Todd conceded, "All right, but I'm the only one who can go in Kristen's lap." At this point, Barry joined the play. But his role was that of a fierce dog. Very dramatically, Barry growled and grimaced. Todd and Cathy, as the two kittens, shrieked fearfully and cuddled close to their mother. Kristen responded, "Oh my babies! Are you scared of the dog?"

This drama was played out several times. Each time, the frightened kittens sought comfort from their mother but there were variations on the central theme. Barry would continue to growl, but one kitten would go out for a walk and say it was lost. Then the other kitten would look for it, find it, and bring it to mommy. Or, both kittens would become lost and mommy would find them.

Was this therapy or educational play? I think both. But by saying it was therapy, I do not mean that we teachers were doing therapy. This kind of play goes on all the time. It is especially prominent in the preschool years. We, then, were simply making it possible for these children to play in preschool ways and, in the process, to become close and become better at coping with feelings by embedding them in play. For these children, such play was just what they needed, in large part because each came from a family troubled by fighting, divorce, and poor parenting practices.

After three months, it was difficult for all of us, teachers and children, to bring our small group to a close. It seemed we had just begun to get into a comfortable groove when it was time to make the transition back to full time in the larger classroom.

That transition happened rather quickly because the time had truly flown by. Toward the very end, we counted down the days on a calendar. Teachers and children talked about what we would miss when our time as a group was over. We talked also about what it would be like to be back full time in the larger classroom. On the last day, we marked the end by having the five children help empty and clean out the room, and the group sang a goodbye song and ate a treat together.

Summary and Conclusion

So, was the experiment a success? If the measure is "Did it cure?" then the answer is no. Most of the serious problem behaviors continued. But if a different, more sensible standard is used, then the experiment was indeed a success. We could see results in the children's attachments to us and in the way they played. They found ways to continue the play themes begun in the small group. Most important, they now could play longer and get more out of play. Barry is a good example.

Before the small group, Barry had been the child who struggled most with friendships. His poor play skills, quick temper, and reluctance to share control prevented him from making friends. But now he could be a reasonably satisfying partner. And, to our surprise, he began to connect with the most popular boy in our class. This boy was popular because of his interests, his fairness, and his enthusiasm for play. He was especially good for Barry because he did not tolerate disruption. In a firm, yet fair manner, he kept Barry in line, much to Barry's (and our) satisfaction. I know this relationship would not have happened before the small group experiment because Barry would not have valued the relationship enough to curb his disruptive ways.

Is the main suggestion here to use a small, "pullout" group for children with serious behavior problems? It is a suggestion, but not, I hope, the main suggestion. The main suggestion is to provide extra support for children with serious behavior problems, support to work on issues we might associate with younger children, particularly support around interactive fantasy play. Thus, the main suggestion, even with young children who have serior problems, is to keep development as the overall aim. By doing so, these children will come to act in kindergarten ways.

12

Developmental Education as Special Education

Kristen J. Willand

*In many ways, this chapter summarizes all that the
book has been about. It does so because here we see
the developmental approach writ large as Kristen Willand recounts her work with Dennis, a very difficult
child with serious attention and behavior problems.
We see the approach in her cultivation of a close relationship with Dennis, in her use of a variety of guidance tactics, in her promotion of play and friendships,
in her use of curriculum, and, most of all, in her
inclusion of Dennis in a classroom community.*

*But we also see that she has more to deal
with than just this child and her classroom. She also
has to deal with a tradition of special education that,
initially, made it more difficult, not easier, to use a
developmental approach. This chapter, then, is about
systemic problems in our schools today, problems that
actually cause behavior problems. It is about different
definitions of special education and different definitions of what it means for children to be included.
Happily, it is also about one school's willingness to
address its systemic problems to make developmental
education a powerful approach to special education.*

W. George Scarlett

In all of my years as a teacher of kindergarten and first grade in both private and public schools, I have encountered many children with special needs and problem behaviors. This chapter focuses on one such child and on how my colleagues and I used a developmental approach to help him. But the chapter also focuses on our struggles to solve systemic problems that threatened to undermine our efforts to help this child, problems arising from a split between our regular classroom's developmental approach and the quite different approach of the special education team. This chapter, then, has a dual focus, one on integrating a child with special needs into a classroom community and the other on integrating special and regular education under a single, developmental approach.

In my early years at the school and at the beginning of one year, there were eight first graders with severe special needs: emotional, behavioral, and learning, mostly some combination of all three. Their education plans determined that these children would have extensive support from the special education staff. A number of specialists and support personnel would be involved, including the speech and language specialist, the guidance counselor, the occupational therapist, the reading specialist, the special education liaison, and two teaching assistants.

The first difficulty arose around the logistics of providing services for eight children. The law required that every effort be made to educate these children in regular classrooms, but to do so created problems of coordinating services. So, to reduce these problems and to provide services as efficiently as possible, we decided to cluster the eight children into just two of the several first-grade classrooms, mine being one of the two.

This decision to cluster the children with special needs prevented placing them with an eye toward creating the right mix. Indeed, in my class, we started the year with the wrong mix. Group meeting times were so bad as to be humorous. Within minutes, several children could not keep their bodies still. They poked, lay down, twirled around, talked out of turn, and did their best to draw others into their games. Those who were not instigators were influenced by instigators to the point where they joined in. Often, the group was out of control.

During these first weeks, we worked hard to establish rules and make ourselves into a group and classroom with reasonable order. Mostly, we worked on basics, such as finding spaces for bodies to go at group times and taking turns. Whole group meeting times were kept short, and at other times children were kept in small groups. Eventually, this work paid off; however, it would not have been necessary had children been placed with an eye toward creating the right mix.

But the biggest difficulty came not around developing order in the classroom but around defining roles for the specialists. Traditionally, special educators have pulled children out of regular classrooms to provide services quite different from what goes on in classrooms. However, pullout methods and segregated special education have led children to feel isolated and confused, hence the push toward inclusion.

Like the special educators, I supported this push. However, initially, my coworkers in special education and I found it difficult to coordinate our efforts and provide services in an integrated way. Initially, our difficulties stemmed from our different histories providing for children with special needs. The push for inclusion was relatively new. Previously, there was a separation between the regular education and special education departments with no specific guidelines for integrating the two. So, as might be expected, the specialists' first attempts at providing services in regular classrooms resembled those from the old, pullout model. The result was that we had difficulties functioning in an integrated way.

For example, one specialist worked with children within our classroom on language-related problems. But rather than working on problems as they occurred naturally in the course of the school day, she worked on them in a separate and formal group. In a similar vein, another specialist used a clearly defined social skills training program in a formal group separate from everyday social situations. And yet another specialist instituted a reading program quite separate and different from the classroom's literature-based program. This reading program offered the clearest example of special education that continues to be separate education, so it warrants a detailed description here.

The reading program was designed to give children skills that the specialist believed were not developed through the regular classroom's curriculum. The nature of this program became evident in the first session I watched, which was near Halloween. In this session, the specialist told the children that she was going to teach them important words they needed to know in order to be able to read. She asked them if they could think what these important words might be. One child said "pumpkin?" and the specialist replied, "Oh no. You're thinking about Halloween. The word pumpkin does not come up a lot in books." "How about ghost?" said another child. "No. You are not thinking. Think about words that you see a lot in books." Eventually, she told the children they would be learning the words *look, come,* and *the.*

As the specialist spoke, the children became visibly frustrated, and Dennis (the child on whom I soon focus in this chapter) began to poke and kick. The rest of the group time was spent trying to manage his and others' problem behaviors. This separate and formal curriculum was not drawing the children in.

For all of these specialists, then, special education still meant separate and formal education, which, from my viewpoint, was not what the children needed. These children needed special education to be integrated with the regular classroom curriculum. Furthermore, they needed a curriculum that encouraged them to be active and invested in what was meaningful and exciting to them. When these needs were not met, the result was behavior problems.

Scheduling, too, became a problem. The specialists were expected to provide services for many children, so their schedules were tight. When they first gave me their schedules, two specialists' times overlapped, which meant there would be too many adults in the classroom at the same time. So, one specialist changed her time, but then her time conflicted with the classroom schedule. Two other specialists gave me back-to-back times, which meant children would be in back-to-back teacher-directed small groups, an arrangement that was sure to produce behavior problems. It was indeed a scheduling mess.

Even when we cleaned up the mess and solved the scheduling problems, there remained problems of timing. Often, one of our classroom activities took longer than expected, so a specialist arrived to work with her small group only to find the children preoccupied and busy. We then had to abruptly stop what we were doing and help the children make a difficult transition. At other times, the specialists got tied up in another classroom and arrived later than expected. This meant the children had to wait, which led to their crawling under tables, poking one another, running around, teasing—in short, disrupting the classroom. The scheduling and timing problems, then, set off behavior problems.

But perhaps the most serious difficulty caused by this segregation of services had to do with the way in which children were perceived. When children are pulled out or placed in formal groups, they often act badly, leading professionals to see them in very negative ways. In contrast, when children are provided services within their regular classrooms where they feel comfortable, they generally act appropriately and come to be seen in very positive ways. This certainly was true in my school. To illustrate this point and to draw attention to how behavior problems can result from segregating children and from perceiving them negatively, here is the story of Dennis.

Dennis

Dennis was a six-year-old boy in my first-grade class. He loved to build with blocks and climb on the playground structures. He loved to play all types of sports (which he did skillfully), and he loved the

Red Sox. He loved to use the computer, and he loved to act, sing, and dance. Dennis also loved to be read to, and, in his classroom, he loved learning how to read. He had a great sense of humor, a wonderful bright smile, and a deep caring for his friends. These were my perceptions from experiencing Dennis in my classroom.

However, they were not the perceptions of others. During much of Dennis's previous school experience, he was perceived negatively by teachers. I heard colleagues talk about Dennis's violent outbursts, his biting of teachers, and his hallway tantrums. I attributed these negative perceptions to his family's state of crisis but also to his separation from his kindergarten classroom. During his kindergarten year, Dennis spent most of his time in a separate room for children with special needs, and when he was in the regular classroom, a teaching assistant from the special education room, Chris, shadowed him. The result was that Dennis never really became included in his regular classroom.

During his kindergarten year and while he was in his regular classroom, I had a chance to observe Dennis. Dennis was in a group of four children led by two special education teachers. Four dividers separated this group from the rest. While I observed, the teachers read from the big book *As the Doorbell Rang*. Dennis's eyes remained glued to the book, and clearly he was entranced by each turn of the page. Each time the doorbell rang in the book, his body bounced. Then, to calm him, Chris would gently put his hand on Dennis's back. The other children also bounced, but because kindergartners typically move their bodies in this way, I did not view Dennis or the other children as acting in anything but normal kindergartner ways. What did seem abnormal was this group's physical separation from the rest of the class. And what did seem abnormal was Dennis being shadowed.

Undoubtedly it was easier for all, including Dennis, to have him receive directions from his own, special education teacher. Yet, this must have confused him. Was this *his* classroom? Were the others *his* teachers? My subsequent observations made the answers to these questions clear.

During free choice time, Dennis chose to use Playdoh, but he remained the only child at a station set up for four. Chris sat or stood next to him, interacting warmly while he worked. And Dennis did indeed work. He pounded, rolled, cut, and sliced the Playdoh. The whole time that he stood, his feet lifted from the floor as his body pressed against the Playdoh. While he made "pizza," he hurriedly moved from one side of the table to the other, putting pizzas in and then taking them out of the "oven." Dennis took cues from Chris about how to extend his play. When Chris said, "Oh, I like my pizza with meatballs," he quickly made Playdoh meatballs and added them to his pizza.

Surely, this experience was valuable for him. In this co-play, he developed skills for play. But how much good is co-play if a child never gets to practice new skills with peers? No other children entered this play. In fact, several children walked by the table, paused, and looked as if they wanted to use the Playdoh, but then they went away. They seemed hesitant, even afraid, to join Dennis at the table. Even when Chris invited them to stay, they went away.

As sad as these observations seemed to me, my observation of Dennis's exit from the classroom seemed even sadder. The classroom teacher had called "cleanup time," and Chris said, "Okay, Dennis, you did a good job today. It's time for us to go back. You can go to the Treasure Box when we get there." While the other children and teachers busied themselves cleaning *their* classroom, Dennis and Chris just left. Apparently, since this classroom was not really Dennis's classroom, cleanup was not part of his routine. Furthermore, no one, no teacher and no child, noticed him or said good-bye. These teachers, then, were not Dennis's teachers, and these classmates were not Dennis's classmates. Certainly, no one there was his friend. I concluded from these observations that for Dennis's next year, we needed to make very different plans.

In planning for the fall, teachers who had worked with Dennis gave me descriptions of his difficult family history, his violent, impulsive behaviors, and his significant language delays. I learned about his biting teachers, his hurting peers, his classmates' fearing him, and his serious problems paying attention. And I learned of his being diagnosed as "having" attention deficit-hyperactivity disorder.

Although I found this background information crucial to seeing his whole picture, I was struck by its being all negative. And even my asking for positive information did not help. When I asked one of the teachers what Dennis especially liked, was interested in, and showed strengths in doing, he paused and said, "Well, he seems to like books, but he can't focus on them for very long." It was obvious that I would have to wait to find answers on my own.

During these planning sessions, all of us agreed that Dennis should continue to have a wide range of special services. But I asked that we begin the school year with a different, more integrated system. I asked that whenever possible, services be provided for Dennis within the regular classroom and I asked that Dennis not be shadowed.

To my relief, the others agreed to these changes. The head teacher of the special education classroom, Mrs. Alexander, and I agreed that, to start the year, no teacher from her room would shadow Dennis. We agreed that if Dennis hurt anyone, he would immediately have to leave the classroom and return only as soon as he was able. And we agreed that someone from her room or I would be on the playground during recess, when Dennis was known to have a difficult time.

From the beginning of the school year, it was obvious that Dennis needed first and foremost a secure base. Because Chris had left, Dennis had no one, and from the start, he mistrusted us. He avoided eye contact and otherwise kept his distance from teachers.

To win his trust, I offered lots of positive feedback. I did so gently but consistently. And I quickly focused on his special skills and interests, particularly his interest in the computer. With time, I was able to tell him, "You are becoming such an expert on the computer," and to tell his classmates, "If you need help with the computer, ask Dennis. He knows all about how to use those games." Aided by such support, Dennis began to make eye contact with me and show pleasure at my compliments. Eventually, each time I complimented his efforts and achievements, his slight smiles grew into full-fledged (toothless) smiles indicating that he was clearly proud of himself and that he was beginning to trust me. I also gained his trust by giving him the message that no matter what inappropriate behaviors he manifested, I would be on his side.

Gaining his trust was helped by our making certain agreements. For example, he agreed that if he hurt anyone, he would have to leave the classroom to take a break in Mrs. Alexander's room. I coupled this agreement with my making explicit that I was his teacher and that because my classroom was his classroom, this was where he belonged.

In the beginning, Dennis tested our relationship and agreements. For example, during the first week, once while Dennis worked at the computer with another child, he refused to give the other child a turn. And when she pleaded her case, Dennis punched her in the arm, which prompted my instigating the usual talk about what could have been accomplished using words instead of fists. After this talk, I reminded Dennis of the agreement about leaving the room if he hurt someone. As I spoke, I tried to be as empathic as possible, with my face and tone of voice as well as with my words. And I tried to show that I was as upset as he was over his having to leave the classroom:

"Do you remember what we decided would happen if you hurt anyone?" He nodded and remained serious as I continued. "Now I have to call Mrs. Alexander because that's what we agreed to do if this happened. But this is your classroom, and this is where you belong. And we're right in the middle of math workshop. I know you really like it, and you're so good at that math computer game. And now you're going to have to miss your time there. I am very sad that you have to miss the rest of math workshop. I hope you calm down very quickly with Mrs. Alexander so that you don't miss anything else. This is where you belong."

Dennis said nothing but watched me intently. Then he followed me quietly to the telephone. We waited by the door for Mrs. Alexander; I repeated to her what I had said to him.

Later, Mrs. Alexander told me that while Dennis was in her room, he just cried and repeated that he wanted to return to our classroom. After a short time, he did return, and I greeted him warmly. I was impressed by how seriously he had taken his consequence. Several weeks later, when the same thing happened, I responded in the same way, as did he. After that, he never again hurt anyone in our classroom. He tested our trust and found he did indeed belong.

So, after spending several months giving him a great deal of time and positive attention, Dennis and I formed a close relationship. Gradually, he sought me out to express his needs, which, for him, was a great improvement. However, it produced a new problem: now, Dennis would not make use of the other adults in his school life. For example, about three months into the school year, during lunchtime, I was eating in the teachers' room when there came a loud knock on the door. Someone opened it; I looked up, and there was Dennis. He was holding a tooth, the first of his baby teeth to fall out. He did not know what to do about the blood in his mouth. Although the cafeteria was filled with staff and parent volunteers, he felt it necessary to seek me out. After I helped him rinse his mouth and find a way to keep his tooth safe, I pointed out all the people in the cafeteria who would have been glad to help.

This same issue of his not using other adults came up with the inclusion specialists. Most of the specialists worked with Dennis in small groups, and, in those groups, Dennis was uncooperative and inattentive. In the middle of the groups, he would often just get up and leave. And if he needed to use the bathroom, he would go to me for permission. I would always say, "Thanks for letting me know you need to use the bathroom," but then I would redirect him to his group's teacher with "but right now you are in Miss Capp's group, and you need to ask her if you can use the bathroom." The specialists became frustrated.

One specialist, in particular, became frustrated by the way Dennis ignored her. She took his reactions personally, which made it more difficult for her to be positive with Dennis. For example, once, while she was involved in our cleanup time, she and Dennis locked horns. Dennis had joined in the cleanup, though he had done so while spinning his body. At one point, he paused to look at the classroom schedule and saw that the next activity was writing. To prepare for writing and while the others were cleaning, he went to the art shelf, took a basket of craypas, and put it on his desk. He had wanted to be sure he would get to use the craypas during writing time.

Not realizing the reason for why Dennis was doing what he was doing, the specialist said in a firm voice, "Dennis, put those craypas back. It's cleanup time." He ignored her, which elicited a much harsher tone: "Dennis, I am speaking to you. Put those craypas back right now! It's cleanup time." Dennis turned his back and walked away. The specialist then walked directly over to him and raised her voice to say, "Dennis! Don't turn your back to me! Go put those away! I've asked you three times!" By now, children were watching, and Dennis looked embarrassed. Then with an angry look, he screamed, "NO!" The specialist replied harshly, "Don't talk back to me!" and so it went until I helped Dennis explain that he was getting the craypas in order to be ready for writing workshop. Because I had waited too long, Dennis had withdrawn. The specialist then said, "All you had to do was tell me that, Dennis."

But that was not so easy for Dennis. First, he had problems communicating. Second, he had problems trusting teachers. Most children respond to teachers simply because they are adults, but not Dennis. Dennis required much more. In particular, he required a continuous positive way of relating before he would respond. I saw it as the teacher's responsibility to figure out how to be positive with

Dennis and create the conditions for trust because, clearly, Dennis could not trust on his own.

As the year progressed, Dennis opened up and became cooperative with those adults who gave him the kind of positive responses he needed. He remained uncooperative with those adults who continued to respond negatively to him.

Besides working on helping Dennis develop trusting and positive relationships with adults, I worked hard to help Dennis connect with his classmates. Given my previous observations of his isolation while in kindergarten, I knew this help was crucial. First, I sought to find what it was that was separating him from the group. Several things became obvious.

The first thing was the way Dennis used his body. He moved around a lot and showed a strong need to touch. This moving around was symptomatic of his attention disorder, but his touching was not. For example, he would walk down the hallway and hip-check all the lockers, and when in the classroom, he would walk from one end of the room to the other, touching every shelf, book, desk, and person along the way. Sometimes Dennis's touching knocked things over, and sometimes it simply surprised, even frightened others. Clearly, his touching was a major reason why others avoided him.

For example, one day early in the school year, Dennis got up from his desk to get colored pencils kept on a shelf across the room and used for illustrating in writing journals. Rather than maneuver between desks, chairs, and people, as children usually do, Dennis took the shortest route by climbing on top of empty chairs and not-so-empty desks, seemingly unaware that his climbing might be scary. I approached him and said, "That's a great idea to use colored pencils for your journal. And you got them all by yourself, good thinking. I noticed that you walked straight here from your seat, but to do that your feet had to step on chairs and desks. And I noticed that when your feet stepped on Jay's desk, he got worried." "But I didn't hurt him," Dennis replied. "You didn't mean to hurt him, but you might have hurt him by accident. Jay, were you surprised to see Dennis's feet on your desk?" "Yeah," said Jay, who had indeed looked very surprised and scared. "You know, Dennis was trying to find the quickest way to get the colored pencils. He didn't mean to scare you," I replied.

During this brief conversation between Jay and me, Dennis watched intently. Then I said, "Let's see if Dennis can find a short way back to his seat keeping his feet on the floor." He did so, and I praised him. He smiled. This was just one example of many where Dennis needed gentle help directing his body and becoming aware of how his body can affect others. In front of the other children, I gave direction as positively as I could, showing the others that there were reasons behind Dennis's movements and that they need not be so frightened. I wanted them to know that I completely accepted Dennis as a member of the group and that I hoped they would accept him too.

Dennis also needed help to develop skills for cooperative play. Here is an example of the kind of help he received:

While playing in the block area with several other children, Dennis needed blocks the others had used in their buildings. Rather than ask the children for the blocks, he proceeded to pull blocks off of their buildings, causing them to collapse. The children were very upset, and they showed it by leaving the block area so that Dennis was now all alone. Dennis then approached me and said, "No one wants to play with me." He hadn't made the connection between his taking the others' blocks and their leaving him, so I walked him through each step of what had happened until he had a sense of the connection.

Soon after this incident, another child, Brent, began playing alongside Dennis in the block area. Once again, Dennis needed another child's blocks, and, once again, he began to reach, not ask. I intervened and reminded him of what happened before, saying, "Do you remember what happened when you took Julia's and Jim's blocks?" He paused and looked at me. "They left," he said. "And you were feeling really sad and lonely in the block area all by yourself. Maybe you can make a better choice about what to do about these blocks so that Brent will want to stay and play with you." With that, he asked Brent if he could use some of his blocks. When Brent explained why he needed the blocks to stay where they were, Dennis, though disappointed, chose different blocks. But to Dennis's satisfaction, Brent stayed and played with him for quite a long time.

In this example, Dennis learned something about what it takes to sustain play with other children. It was in real situations such as these rather than in formal, separate groups where Dennis learned how to become a fair player.

It was also necessary to address Dennis's bear-hug, "pick-you-up" greetings, which he gave at the start of the day. In the morning, Dennis would enter the classroom, come up to children from behind, grab them, lift them up off the ground, and say hello. Some were amused, but others were scared or uncomfortable, resulting usually in their saying "Dennnnnissss!" in a loud and annoyed way.

When this happened, I intervened to help the children tell Dennis exactly what they wanted him to do. I told them he was a good listener. One child, Carol, said in a reasonable tone, "Put me down," and Dennis did. I praised them both for the way they spoke and listened to each other. The reason this worked was that Dennis really did want to please. He cared deeply about being part of this peer group, so he worked hard to listen.

But of all the tactics for helping Dennis connect with his classmates, reframing was the most helpful. Here is an example:

One day, as we were getting ready to go home from school, I was handing out children's homework packets one at a time, reading the children's names for them to come and take their packets home. Dennis stood nearby. Just as I began to read a child's name on one packet, Dennis loudly read the name on the next. Not only was it hard for the children to hear their names, it was also slowing down our transition home. I sensed that the children were getting annoyed. After the third packet, I said, "Dennis, you are such a good reader, you are reading every person's name beautifully." He smiled, and there was a sense of relief in the classroom. I then allowed him to read the names on the rest of the packets.

Group meeting times have offered many opportunities for reframing. For example, we had been studying Bill Martin, Jr.'s (the author of *Chicka Chicka Boom Boom*) literature, and we had talked a lot about the rhythm in his books. One morning, while we all gathered in the group area to read one of Martin's books, Dennis was having particular difficulty keeping his body calm. In the middle of the book, Dennis stood up and began dancing to the rhythm of the words. I said, "His words really do make you feel like dancing. Whenever I get to this repeating verse, everyone can stand up and dance to the rhythm of it."

In order to help Dennis become part of the group, I had to do everything possible to make the children see Dennis in a positive light. And often this meant reinterpreting the things Dennis did that made him different from the rest. However, at other times it meant finding ways for Dennis to be just like the rest. This was especially important at group meeting times.

Group meeting times serve several crucial functions: they gather our whole class together and they allow us to exchange messages, think about our daily schedule, learn about new choices, and play group games. One simply had to be part of our group meeting times in order to be part of our group. Because he had initially been so disruptive in kindergarten, Dennis had not been expected to sit through group meeting times. However, in my class, Dennis was expected to sit through group meeting times because these times are crucial to the formation of a community.

As I have already indicated, this particular group had a very hard time coming together at the beginning of the school year. But with work, they got better. Part of this work involved children coming up with strategies that would help them participate better. For example, one child whose body flopped up and down throughout group time decided it would help him focus better if he sat on the floor. It did help. Dennis decided he would do better if he sat close to me. The group supported this decision, and it too helped.

Once Dennis could play with others and once he became part of the group, he needed help making friends. I helped him in several ways, one being building on his interest in the computer and in computer games. He had a real fascination with the computer and was skillful at figuring out how new games worked. I decided I would teach him how to put the disks in, set up certain games, and play games that he could, in turn, teach others. After a while, if someone else could not figure out how to start a new game, I directed the child to Dennis. Soon, Dennis became the class computer expert, the resource children went to when they had a problem. And because Dennis would stay and figure out their problems, children began to see Dennis more as their friend.

I also worked with Dennis on ways to enter others' play. At the beginning of the year, when he wanted to join a group at play with blocks, he would often walk over to the group, circle their structure, and almost tip it over. This usually elicited a "Dennniiisss!!" After some coaching, Dennis became better able to approach a group and say simply, "Can I play too?" The best thing about this change was that, in time, the answer from the other children was "Sure!"

Another area where I worked hard to help Dennis connect to the classroom was curriculum. My first observations of Dennis using Playdoh made me think that the curriculum could be a powerful tool for managing his behavior. And, happily, that proved to be the case. From the beginning of the year, Dennis was totally excited about books and our projects. However, because of his high activity level, he needed active learning with high levels of stimulation.

In the everyday life of the classroom, Dennis was completely invested in literature. He made excellent observations about authors, illustrations, and stories, and he often chose to look at books on his own. He was completely attentive while being read to, and he demonstrated a real enjoyment of literature.

During our study of African literature, Dennis chose to work in a small group creating a play based on one of his favorite African tales. Because Dennis loved to act and because he loved the tale, he quickly connected with the process and stayed invested for the forty-five minutes of reading workshop for three consecutive days. Dennis and the other group members used the book for reference to figure out the sequence of acts. They also used the book to determine the most important pieces of the story. In addition, they helped one another find their parts in the book so that they could all practice. Even though Dennis knew the book very well, he had to work hard to read and reread his parts until he understood when and how to say his lines. He and the others also created simple costumes and discussed how best to represent the characters. The culmination of this lengthy process was a performance in front of the class. Throughout, Dennis was highly motivated and invested, and because of that, he behaved appropriately. He also learned a lot about literacy.

In December, we had Dennis's midyear review meeting. I went first and talked about all the wonderful progress Dennis was making. I talked about the effort and attention he needed from us and about our strategies for helping him feel secure, find a place in the group, and participate in the curriculum. I concluded by saying that the current situation was working and that we should continue to see him progress.

After the meeting, one person stopped me in the hallway. She said, "I am completely floored by what you said about Dennis. Is he really functioning like that in the classroom? I tested him last year. Well, I tried to test him. I have had all kinds, and I almost always get them to respond somewhat to the tasks, but Dennis was completely out of control. He ran around the room and refused to cooperate. I was sure that this meeting was to recommend an outside placement."

How sad. My heart sank to think that outside treatment had even been a possibility for Dennis. And I shudder to think what would have happened had he been placed in a classroom that did not build on his strengths and interests and did not help him connect to others. Would he have been sent away for outside treatment or otherwise kept in an abnormal environment? I worry that this happens too often with children like Dennis.

Certainly, there are cases so severe that they need drastic responses such as outside treatment. However, despite his previous negative profile, his background, his attention deficit-hyperactivity disorder, and his serious behavior problems, Dennis was not such a case—for the simple reason that he was thriving in a regular classroom.

As the year went on and as Dennis became more a part of the classroom community, the contrast between his behavior in regular classroom activities and his behavior in segregated small groups became increasingly apparent. One of the special education teachers noticed the contrast. She noticed that during his regular classroom's writing time, Dennis was invested, focused, and appropriate in his behavior. As a result of her noticing, she began to use the regular classroom's literature as the basis for her own work with Dennis. She was rewarded when Dennis became more responsive in her groups.

In the following school year, this same special educator worked again with children in my classroom. But this time she began the year with a much more integrated program. And as the school year progressed, she became wonderfully open to working with children on projects that extended from the regular classroom's literature. Happily, this example was not unique.

As Dennis moved on to second grade, those providing him with special services now understood his strong need to be a part of the classroom community. As a result, they abandoned much in their old approach that had contributed to his problem behaviors. So, for example, rather than working with Dennis in a separate small group to develop social skills, they held meetings with the class as a whole on social issues that directly related to Dennis and others.

It is important to note that all these changes did not occur simply from educators noticing improvement. They occurred also because changes were made in how the special educators worked with classroom teachers. The most important change may have been our principal providing us with time for monthly group and weekly individual meetings between special educators and classroom teachers, time we needed in order to plan effectively for how best to work together.

Certainly, with Dennis, we worked best when all of us adopted a developmental approach to his behavior problems, when we worked to make him feel a part of the classroom community, when we helped him learn within the context of everyday classroom life, and when we provided curriculum that had real meaning for him. And, certainly, we worked best when instead of treating Dennis as if he were defective or deficient, we treated him as a growing, developing child.

· ·

Conclusion
The Long-Term View

*The heartbreaking difficulty in pedagogy . . . is the
fact that the best methods are also the most difficult
ones.*

Jean Piaget (1977, p. 712)

Piaget is right. The best methods are the most difficult ones. And
so, with a developmental approach to behavior problems, there
comes a price, a price from having to address so many problems at
once. How simple it would be if forcing children to behave was the
cure for behavior problems. How simple it would be if focusing on
problem behaviors was all that mattered. But if there is any one
thing this book tries to show, it is that behavior problems cannot
be resolved simply by controlling children or by managing problem
behaviors. However, because a developmental approach is so complex, there can come times when it all seems too much, when the
approach itself threatens a meltdown.

This point about complexity and meltdown became clear to me
during one painful workshop experience. To a group of kindergarten
and first-grade teachers from a troubled inner-city school, I was
going on and on about developing partnerships with children and
going on and on about sharing control, when one teacher could
stand it no longer. She jumped to her feet in anger and accused me
of missing the point. Her point was that she was desperate. Her

point was that in her classroom she was alone with too many students, many of whom had serious emotional problems. It is all fine and dandy, she said, to talk about supporting development, except when the ship's going down.

The demands and limitations of a developmental approach also hit home to me while consulting around a pair of twin four-year-old boys. These boys regularly wreaked havoc in the classroom. They fought. They destroyed toys. They disobeyed teachers. Their two teachers worked patiently to develop attachments; they supported the boys' constructive play. They built curriculum on the boys' interests in superheroes, and they led fine discussions about classroom rules. In short, they did everything that good developmental educators should do. And yet, the behavior problems continued. Yes, there was progress. Over time, the boys did fit more into the community, did play more constructively, and did begin to make friends. But the progress was painfully slow.

Part of the reason it was so slow was the boys' mother. The mother's personal life was a shambles, and, unfortunately, she took some of her anger and unhappiness out on the school. She missed appointments with the school's director and told the boys they need not listen to their teachers.

In this difficult situation, the teachers found themselves becoming increasingly exhausted. Compounding the problem, one of the teachers had a serious, chronic illness that drained her energies on even the best of days. I worried about the boys and the classroom, but I also worried about the teachers and their stress. So, I suggested the teachers take a different approach, one that would at least temporarily ignore supporting long-term development and focus on gaining control.

The teachers understood my concern but decided not to give up on a developmental approach. They felt that there was strength in these boys and that a developmental approach allowed them to build on this strength. They felt that switching to a program designed simply to control would undermine all their hard work to support normal development in these boys. So, there we were, in an ironic switch of the usual roles. In retrospect, they proved to be much stronger than me. They stuck to a developmental approach and paid a heavy price for doing so. But I think they did right. No miracles happened, but there was progress, however slow.

Fortunately, these times are rare when classrooms and teachers risk collapsing under the weight of a developmental approach. But they do occur, and they remind us that in order for a developmental approach to work well, programs must have at least minimal supports and resources, and teachers must have more than minimal patience and capacity to care.

But, really, why should we care so much? Other, simpler approaches might well be enough. Time-out, praising good behavior, giving warnings around transitions—in short, tried-and-true tactics for managing problem behaviors might be enough for maintaining order and create at least some room for development. Why should we overspend for a new Cadillac when a used Chevy would better fit our budget and do almost as well?

My answer to this question of why we should expend so much time, thought, and energy on a developmental approach to behavior problems is that children will do much better in the end. This generation of young children depends on teachers. With women now commonly in the work force, with so many single-parent families, and with the influx of new immigrant groups without money, families today look to early childhood programs to share in the task of child rearing. What is being bought, then, is not a Cadillac or Chevy but the support our young children need to optimally grow.

Furthermore, many families do not know how to develop partnerships with children or how to share control. Too often we find parents spanking and yelling or otherwise trying to overcontrol their children. And too often we find just the opposite: parents not setting limits when they should be and otherwise resorting to undercontrol. Good teachers, then, may be many children's best hope for developing self-control.

The point here is not that early childhood educators must solve all domestic problems. The point here is that a teacher's work goes far beyond the classroom's walls. Today's parents need help raising young children, more help than perhaps at any time before. And today's young children need help to develop, more help than parents can give. If teachers do not provide that help, who will?

References

Ballenger, C. "Because You Like Us: The Language of Control." *Harvard Educational Review*, 1992, *62*(2), 199–208.

DeVries, R., and Kohlberg, L. *Constructivist Early Education: Overview and Comparison with Other Programs.* Washington, D.C.: National Association for the Education of Young Children, 1990.

Dewey, J. *Experience and Education.* New York: Macmillan and Kappa Delta Pi, an International Honor Society in Education, 1963.

Dreikurs, R., and Grey, L. *The New Approach to Discipline: Logical Consequences.* New York: Dutton, 1990.

Eckerman, C., Whatley, J., and Kutz, S. "Growth of Social Play with Peers During the Second Year of Life." *Developmental Psychology*, 1975, *11*, 42–49.

Erikson, E. *Childhood and Society.* New York: Norton, 1950.

Erikson, E. *Young Man Luther.* New York: Norton, 1962.

Essa, E. *Practical Guide to Solving Preschool Behavior Problems.* Albany, N.Y.: Delmar, 1983.

Freud, A. "The Concept of Developmental Lines." In R. Eissler, A. Freud, H. Hartmann, and M. Kris (eds.), *The Psychoanalytic Study of the Child.* Vol. 18. Madison, Conn.: International Universities Press, 1963.

Gould, R. *Child Studies Through Fantasy.* New York: Quadrangle Books, 1972.

Greenberg, M., and Speltz, M. "Attachment and the Ontogeny of Conduct Problems." In J. Belsky and T. Nezworsk (eds.), *Clinical Implications of Attachment.* Hillside, N.J.: Erlbaum, 1988.

Honig, A. *Love and Learn: Discipline for Young Children.* Washington, D.C.: National Association for the Education of Young Children, 1989.

"Ideas That Work with Young Children." *Young Children*, 1988, *44*(1), 25.

Katz, L. "Mothering and Teaching: Some Significant Distinctions." In *Current Topics in Early Childhood.* Norwood, N.J.: Ablex, 1988.

Kohlberg, L., and Mayer, R. "Development as the Aim of Education." *Harvard Educational Review*, 1972, *42*(4), 449–496. Copyright © 1972 by the President and Fellows of Harvard College. All rights reserved.

Lewis, M., and Rosenblum, L. (eds.), *Friendship and Peer Relations*. New York: Wiley, 1975.

Mahler, M., Pine, F., and Bergman, A. *Psychological Birth of the Human Infant: Symbiosis and Individuation*. New York: Basic Books, 1975.

Marion, M. *Guidance of Young Children*. (2nd ed.) Columbus, Ohio: Merrill, 1987.

Mitchell, G. *Help! What Do I Do About . . .* New York: Scholastic, 1993.

Moore, G. T. "The Physical Environment and Cognitive Development in Child-Care Centers." In C. Weinstein and T. David (eds.), *Spaces for Children*. New York: Plenum, 1987.

Mueller, E. "The Maintenance of Verbal Exchanges Between Young Children." *Child Development*, 1972, *43*, 930–938.

Piaget, J. *Science of Education and the Psychology of the Child*. New York: Grossman, 1970.

Piaget, J. "Development of Teaching Methods." In H. Gruber and J. Voneche (eds.), *The Essential Piaget*. New York: Basic Books, 1977.

Redl, F., and Wineman, D. *Controls from Within*. New York: Free Press, 1965.

Rubin, K. *Children's Friendships*. Cambridge, Mass.: Harvard University Press, 1980.

Ryle, G. *The Concept of Mind*. London: Hutchinson, 1949.

Scarlett, W. G. "Social Isolation from Agemates Among Nursery School Children." *Journal of Child Psychology and Psychiatry*, 1980, *21*(3), 231–235.

Scarlett, W. G. "Co-Playing: Teachers as Models for Friendship." In D. Wolf (ed.), *Connecting: Friendship in the Lives of Young Children and Their Teachers*. Redmond, Wash.: Exchange Press, 1986.

Selman, R., and Hickey-Shultz, L. *Making a Friend in Youth*. Chicago: University of Chicago Press, 1990.

Stern, D. *The Interpersonal World of the Infant*. New York: Basic Books, 1985.

Stone, J. *A Guide to Discipline*. Washington, D.C.: National Association for the Education of Young Children, 1994.

Sullivan, H. S. *The Interpersonal Theory of Psychiatry*. New York: Norton, 1953.

Weinstein, C. "Designing Preschool Classrooms to Support Development: Research and Reflection." In C. Weinstein and T. David (eds.), *Spaces for Children*. New York: Plenum, 1987.

Wilder, L. I. *On the Banks of Plum Creek*. New York: HarperCollins, 1965. (Originally published 1937.)

Index